A street of Puebla, Mexico, and the Soledad Church

TRAMPING THROUGH MEXICO, GUATEMALA AND HONDURAS

Being the Random Notes
of an Incurable Vagabond

BY

HARRY A. FRANCK

Author of "A Vagabond Journey Around
the World," "Zone Policeman
88," etc.

ILLUSTRATED WITH PHOTOGRAPHS
BY THE AUTHOR

NEW YORK
THE CENTURY CO.
1916

TO
THE MEXICAN PEON
WITH
SINCEREST WISHES
FOR HIS
ULTIMATE EMANCIPATION

FOREWORD

This simple story of a journey southward grew up of itself. Planning a comprehensive exploration of South America, I concluded to reach that continent by some less monotonous route than the steamship's track; and herewith is presented the unadorned narrative of what I saw on the way,— the day-by-day experiences in rambling over bad roads and into worse lodging-places that infallibly befall all who venture afield south of the Rio Grande. The present account joins up with that of five months on the Canal Zone, already published, clearing the stage for a larger forthcoming volume on South America giving the concrete results of four unbroken years of Latin-American travel.

HARRY A. FRANCK.

New York, May, 1916.

TABLE OF CONTENTS

LIST OF ILLUSTRATIONS

LIST OF ILLUSTRATIONS

LIST OF ILLUSTRATIONS

LIST OF ILLUSTRATIONS

TRAMPING THROUGH
MEXICO, GUATEMALA
AND HONDURAS

TRAMPING THROUGH MEXICO, GUATEMALA AND HONDURAS

CHAPTER I

INTO THE COOLER SOUTH

YOU are really in Mexico before you get there. Laredo is a purely — though not pure — Mexican town with a slight American tinge. Scores of dull-skinned men wander listlessly about trying to sell sticks of candy and the like from boards carried on their heads. There are not a dozen shops where the clerks speak even good pidgin English, most signs are in Spanish, the lists of voters on the walls are chiefly of Iberian origin, the very county officers from sheriff down — or up — are names the average American could not pronounce, and the saunterer in the streets may pass hours without hearing a word of English. Even the post-office employees speak Spanish by preference and I could not do the simplest business without resorting to that tongue. I am fond of Spanish, but I do not relish being forced to use it in my own country.

3

On Laredo's rare breeze rides enough dust to build
a new world.   Every street is inches deep in it,
everything in town, including the minds of the inhabitants, is covered with it.   As to heat —" Cin-
cinnati Slim" put it in a nutshell even as we
wandered in from the cattleyards where the freight
train had dropped us in the small hours: "If ever
hell gets full this 'll do fine for an annex."

Luckily my window in the ruin that masqueraded
as a hotel faced such wind as existed.   The only
person I saw in that institution during twenty-four
hours there was a little Mexican boy with a hand-
broom, which he evidently carried as an ornament
or a sign of office.   It seemed a pity not to let
Mexico have the dust-laden, sweltering place if they
want it so badly.

I had not intended to lug into Mexico such a load
as I did.   But it was a Jewish holiday, and the
pawnshops were closed.   As I passed the lodge on
the north end of the bridge over the languid, brown
Rio Grande it was a genuine American voice that
snapped: "Heh!   A nickel!"

Just beyond, but thirty-six minutes earlier, the
Mexican official stopped me with far more courtesy,
and peered down into the corners of my battered
" telescope " without disturbing the contents.

" Monterey? " he asked.

" Sí, señor."

" No revólver? " he queried suspiciously.

The first glimpse of Mexico. Looking across the Rio Grande at
Laredo

A corner of Monterey from my hotel window

"No, señor," I answered, keeping the coat on my arm unostentatiously over my hip pocket. It was n't a revolver; it was an automatic.

The man who baedekerized Mexico says Nuevo Laredo is not the place to judge that country. I was glad to hear it. Its imitation of a street-car, eight feet long, was manned by two tawny children without uniforms, nor any great amount of substitute for them, who smoked cigarettes incessantly as we crawled dustily through the baked-mud hamlet to the decrepit shed that announced itself the station of the National Railways of Mexico. It was closed, of course. I waited an hour or more before two officials resplendent in uniforms drifted in to take up the waiting where I had left off. But it was a real train that pulled in toward three, from far-off St. Louis, even if it had hooked on behind a second-class car with long wooden benches.

For an hour we rambled across just such land as southern Texas, endless flat sand scattered with chaparral, mesquite, and cactus; nowhere a sign of life, but for fences of one or two barb-wires on crooked sticks — not even bird life. The wind, strong and incessant as at sea, sounded as mournful through the thorny mesquite bushes as in our Northern winters, even though here it brought relief rather than suffering. The sunshine was unbrokenly glorious.

Benches of stained wood in two-inch strips ran

the entire length of our car, made in Indiana. In the center were ten double back-to-back seats of the same material. The conductor was American, but as in Texas he seemed to have little to do except to keep the train moving. The auditor, brakeman, and train-boy were Mexicans, in similar uniforms, but of thinner physique and more brown of color. The former spoke fluent English. The engineer was American and the fireman a Negro.

Far ahead, on either side, hazy high mountains appeared, as at sea. By the time we halted at Lampazos, fine serrated ranges stood not far distant on either hand. From the east came a never-ceasing wind, stronger than that of the train, laden with a fine sand that crept in everywhere. Mexican costumes had appeared at the very edge of the border; now there were even a few police under enormous hats, with tight trousers and short jackets showing a huge revolver at the hip. Toward evening things grew somewhat greener. A tree six to twelve feet high, without branches, or sometimes with several trunk-like ones, growing larger from bottom to top and ending in a bristling bunch of leaves, became common. The mountains on both sides showed fantastic peaks and ridges, changing often in aspect; some, thousands of feet high with flat tableland tops, others in strange forms the imagination could animate into all manner of creatures.

A goatherd, wild, tawny, bearded, dressed in sun-faded sheepskin, was seen now and then tending his flocks of little white goats in the sand and cactus. This was said to be the rainy season in northern Mexico. What must it be in the dry?

Toward five the sun set long before sunset, so high was the mountain wall on our right. The sand-storm had died down, and the sand gave way to rocks. The moon, almost full, already smiled down upon us over the wall on the left. We continued along the plain between the ranges, which later receded into the distance, as if retiring for the night. Flat, mud-colored, Palestinian adobe huts stood here and there in the moonlight among patches of a sort of palm bush.

Monterey proved quite a city. Yet how the ways of the Spaniard appeared even here! Close as it is to the United States, with many American residents and much " americanizado," according to the Mexican, the city is in architecture, arrangement, customs, just what it would be a hundred miles from Madrid; almost every little detail of life is that of Spain, with scarcely enough difference to suggest another country, to say nothing of another hemisphere. England brings to her colonies some of her home customs, but not an iota of what Spain does to the lands she has conquered. The hiding of wealth behind a miserable façade is almost as universal in Mexico of the twentieth century as in

Morocco of the fourth. The narrow streets of Monterey have totally inadequate sidewalks on which two pedestrians pass, if at all, with the rubbing of shoulders. Outwardly the long vista of bare house fronts that toe them on either side are dreary and poor, every window barred as those of a prison. Yet in them sat well-dressed señoritas waiting for the lovers who "play the bear" to late hours of the night, and over their shoulders the passerby caught many a glimpse of richly furnished rooms and flowery patios beyond.

The river Catalina was drier than even the Manzanares, its rocky bed, wide enough to hold the upper Connecticut, entirely taken up by mule and donkey paths and set with the cloth booths of fruit sellers. As one moves south it grows cooler, and Monterey, fifteen hundred feet above sea-level, was not so weighty in its heat as Laredo and southern Texas. But, on the other hand, being surrounded on most sides by mountains, it had less breeze, and the coatless freedom of Texas was here looked down upon. During the hours about noonday the sun seemed to strike physically on the head and back whoever stepped out into it, and the smallest fleck of white cloud gave great and instant relief. From ten to four, more or less, the city was strangely quiet, as if more than half asleep, or away on a vacation, and over it hung that indefinable scent peculiar to Arab and Spanish countries. Compared

A peon restaurant in the market-place of San Luís Potosí

A market woman of San Luís Potosí

with Spain, however, its night life and movement
was slight.

Convicts in perpendicularly striped blue and
white pajamas worked in the streets. That is, they
moved once every twenty minutes or so, usually to
roll a cigarette. They were without shackles, but
several guards in brown uniforms and broad felt
hats, armed with thick-set muskets, their chests
criss-crossed with belts of long rifle cartridges,
lolled in the shade of every near-by street corner.
The prisoners laughed and chatted like men perfectly contented with their lot, and moved about with
great freedom. One came a block to ask me the
time, and loafed there some fifteen minutes before
returning to his " labor."

Mexico is strikingly faithful to its native dress.
Barely across the Rio Grande the traveler sees at
once hundreds of costumes which in any American
city would draw on all the boy population as surely
as the Piper of Hamelin. First and foremost comes
always the enormous hat, commonly of thick felt
with decorative tape, the crown at least a foot high,
the brim surely three feet in diameter even when
turned up sufficient to hold a half gallon of water.
That of the peon is of straw; he too wears the skin-
tight trousers, and goes barefoot but for a flat
leather sandal held by a thong between the big toe
and the rest. In details and color every dress was
as varied and individual as the shades of complexion.

My hotel room had a fine outlook to summer-blue mountains, but was blessed with neither mirror, towel, nor water. I descended to the alleyway between " dining-room " and barnyard, where I had seen the general washbasin, but found the landlady seated on the kitchen floor shelling into it peas for our *almuerzo*. This and the evening *comida* were always identically the same. A cheerful but slatternly Indian woman set before me a thin soup containing a piece of squash and a square of boiled beef, and eight hot corn tortillas of the size and shape of our pancakes, or *gkebis*, the Arab bread, which it outdid in toughness, and totally devoid of taste. Next followed a plate of rice with peppers, a plate of tripe less tough than it should have been, and a plate of brown beans which was known by the name of *chile con carne*, but in which I never succeeded in finding anything carnal. Every meal ended with a cup of the blackest coffee.

Out at the end of calle B a well-worn rocky path leads up to a ruined chapel on the summit of a hill, the famous Obispado from which the city was shelled and taken by the Americans in 1847. Below, Monterey lies flat, with many low trees peering above the whitish houses, all set in a perfectly level plain giving a great sense of roominess, as if it could easily hold ten such cities. At the foot of the hill, some three hundred feet high, is an unoccupied space. Then the city begins, leisurely at first, with few houses and many gardens and trees, thickening farther on. All about are mountains. The Silla (Saddle), a sharp rugged height backing the city on the right, has a notch in it much like the seat of a Texas saddle; to the far left are fantastic sharp peaks, and across the plain a ragged range perhaps fifteen miles distant shuts off the view. Behind the chapel stand Los Dientes, a teeth or saw-like range resembling that behind Lecco in Italy. Only a young beggar and his female mate occupied the ruined chapel, built, like the town, of whitish stone that is soft when dug but hardens upon exposure to the air. They cooked on the littered floor of one of the dozen rooms, and all the walls of the chamber under the great dome were set with pegs for birds, absent now, but which had carpeted the floor with proof of their frequent presence.

At five the sun set over the city, so high is the Dientes range, but for some time still threw a soft light on the farther plain and hills. Compared with our own land there is something profoundly peaceful in this climate and surroundings. Now the sunshine slipped up off the farther ranges, showing only on the light band of clouds high above the farther horizon, and a pale-faced moon began to brighten, heralding a brilliant evening.

Fertile plains of corn stretched south of the city, but already dry, and soon giving way to mesquite and dust again. Mountains never ceased, and lay fantastically heaped up on every side. We rose ever higher, though the train kept a moderate speed. At one station the bleating of a great truck-load of kids, their legs tied, heaped one above the other, was startlingly like the crying of babies. We steamed upward through a narrow pass, the mountains crowding closer on either hand and seeming to grow lower as we rose higher among them. The landscape became less arid, half green, with little or no cactus, and the breeze cooled steadily. Saltillo at last, five thousand feet up, was above the reach of oppressive summer and for perhaps the first time since leaving Chicago I did not suffer from the heat. It was almost a pleasure to splash through the little puddles in its poorly paved streets. Its plazas were completely roofed with trees, the view down any of its streets was enticing, and the little cubes of houses were painted all possible colors without any color scheme whatever. Here I saw the first *pulquerías*, much like cheap saloons in appearance, with swinging doors, sometimes a pool table, and a bartender of the customary I-tell-yer-I 'm-tough physiognomy. Huge earthen jars of the fermented cactus juice stood behind the bar, much like milk in appearance, and was served in glazed pots, size to order. In Mexico *pulquería* stands for saloon and *peluquería* for barber-shop, resulting now and then in sad mistakes by wandering Yankees innocent of Spanish.

Some sold potatoes no larger than nuts

A policeman and an arriero

There were a hundred adult passengers by actual count, to say nothing of babies and unassorted bundles, in the second-class car that carried me on south into the night. Every type of Mexican was represented, from white, soft, city-bred specimens to sturdy countrymen so brown as to be almost black. A few men were in "European" garb. Most of them were dressed á la peón, very tight trousers fitting like long leggings, collarless shirts of all known colors, a gay faja or cloth belt, sometimes a coat — always stopping at the waist. Then last, but never least, the marvelous hat. Two peons trying to get through the same door at once was a sight not soon to be forgotten. There were felt and straw hats of every possible grade and every shade and color except red, wound with a rich band about the crown and another around the brim. Those of straw were of every imaginable weave, some of rattan, like baskets or veranda furniture. The Mexican male seems to be able to endure sameness of costume below it, but unless his hat is individual, life is a drab blank to him. With his hat off the peon loses seven eights of his impressiveness. The women, with only a black sort of thin shawl over their heads, were eminently inconspicuous in the forest of hatted men.

Mournfully out of the black drizzling night about the station came the dismal wails of hawkers at their little stands dim-lighted by pale lanterns; "*Anda*

pulque! " Within the car was more politeness —
or perhaps, more exactly, more unconscious consideration for others than north of the Rio Grande.
There were many women among us, yet all the night
through there was not a suggestion of indecency or
annoyance.   Indian blood largely predominated,
hardy, muscular, bright-eyed fellows, yet in conduct
all were *caballeros*.   Near me sat a family of three.
The father, perhaps twenty, was strikingly handsome in his burnished copper skin, his heavy black
hair, four or five inches long, hanging down in
" bangs " below his hat.   The mother was even
younger, yet the child was already some two years
old, the chubbiest, brightest-eyed bundle of humanity imaginable.   In their fight for a seat the man
shouted to the wife to hand him the child.   He
caught it by one hand and swung it high over two
seats and across the car, yet it never ceased smiling.
The care this untutored fellow took to give wife and
child as much comfort as possible was superior to
that many a " civilized " man would have shown all
night under the same circumstances.   Splendid
teeth were universal among the peons.   There was
no chewing of tobacco, but much spitting by both
sexes.   A delicate, child-like young woman drew out
a bottle and swallowed whole glassfuls of what
I took to be milk, until the scent of pulque, the native
beverage, suddenly reached my nostrils.

The fat brown auditor addressed señora, the

peon's wife, with the highest respect, even if he insisted on doing his duty to the extent of pushing
aside the skirts of the women to peer under the long
wooden bench for passengers. A dispute soon
arose. Fare was demanded of a ragged peon for the
child of three under his arm. The peon shook his
head, smiling. The auditor's voice grew louder.
Still the father smiled silently. The ticket collector
stepped back into the first-class car and returned
with the train guard, a boyish-looking fellow in peon
garb from hat to legging trousers, with a brilliant
red tie, two belts of enormous cartridges about his
waist, in his hand a short ugly rifle, and a harmless smile on his face. There was something fascinating about the stocky little fellow with his half-
embarrassed grin. One felt that of himself he
would do no man hurt, yet that a curt order would
cause him to send one of those long steel-jacketed
bullets through a man and into the mountain side
beyond. Luckily he got no such orders. The auditor pointed out the malefactor, who lost no time
in paying the child's half-fare.

This all-night trip must be done sooner or later
by all who enter Mexico by way of Laredo, for the
St. Louis–Mexico City Limited with its sleeping-car
behind and a few scattered Americans in first-class
is the only one that covers this section. Residents
of Vanegas, for example, who wish to travel south
must be at the station at three in the morning.

Most of the night the train toiled painfully upward. As a man scorns to set out after a hearty meal with a lunch under his arm, so in the swelter of Texas I had felt it foolish to be lugging a bundle of heavy clothing. By midnight I began to credit myself with foresight. The windows were closed, yet the land of yesterday seemed far behind indeed. I wrapped my heavy coat about me. Toward four we crossed the Tropic of Cancer into the Torrid Zone, without a jolt, and I dug out my gray sweater and regretted I had abandoned the old blue one in an empty box-car. Twice I think I drowsed four minutes with head and elbow on my bundle, but except for two or three women who jack-knifed on the long bench no one found room to lie down during the long night.

From daylight on I stood in the vestibule and watched the drab landscape hurry steadily past. No mountains were in sight now because we were on top of them. Yet no one would have suspected from the appearance of the country that we were considerably more than a mile above sea-level. The flat land looked not greatly different from that of the day before. The cactus was higher; some of the "organ" variety, many of the "Spanish bayonet" species, lance-like stalks eight to ten feet high. The rest was bare ground with scattered mesquite bushes. Had I not known the altitude I

might have attributed the slight light-headedness to
a sleepless night.

Certainly a hundred ragged *cargadores*, hotel
runners, and boys eager to carry my bundle attacked
me during my escape from the station of San Luís
Potosí at seven, and there were easily that many
carriages waiting, without a dozen to take them.
The writer of Mexico's Baedeker speaks of the city
as well-to-do. Either it has vastly changed in a
few years or he wrote it up by absent treatment.
Hardly a town of India exceeds it in picturesque
poverty. Such a surging of pauperous humanity,
dirt, and uncomplaining misery I had never before
seen in the Western Hemisphere. Plainly the name
" republic " is no cure for man's ills. The chief
center was the swarming market. Picture a dense
mob of several thousand men and boys, gaunt,
weather-beaten, their tight trousers collections of
rents and patchwork in many colors, sandals of a
soft piece of leather showing a foot cracked, blackened, tough as a hoof, as incrusted with filth as a dead
foot picked up on a garbage heap, the toes always
squirting with mud, the feet not merely never washed
but the sandal never removed until it wears off and
drops of its self. Above this a collarless shirt,
blouse or short jacket, ragged, patched, of many
faded colors, yet still showing half the body. Then
a dull, uncomplaining, take-things-as-they-come

face, unwashed, never shaved — the pure Indian
grows a sort of dark down on his cheeks and the
point of the chin, the half-breeds a slight beard —
all topped by the enormous hat, never missing,
though often full of holes, black with dirt, weather-
beaten beyond expression.

Then there were fully as many women and girls,
even less fortunate, for they had not even sandals,
but splashed along barefoot among the small cold
cobblestones. Their dress seemed gleaned from a
rag-heap and their heads were bare, their black hair
combed or plastered flat. Children of both sexes
were exact miniatures of their elders. All these
wretches were here to sell. Yet what was for sale
could easily have been tended by twenty persons.
Instead, every man, woman, and child had his own
stand, or bit of cloth or cobblestone on which to
spread a few scanty, bedraggled wares. Such a
mass of silly, useless, pathetic articles, toy jars, old
bottles, anything that could be found in all the
dump-heaps of Christendom. The covered market
housed only a very small percentage of the whole.
There was a constant, multicolored going and coming, with many laden asses and miserable, gaunt
creatures bent nearly double under enormous loads
on head or shoulders. Every radiating narrow
mud-dripping street for a quarter-mile was covered
in all but the slight passageway in the center with
these displays. Bedraggled women sat on the

cobbles with aprons spread out and on them little
piles of six nuts each, sold at a centavo. There
were peanuts, narrow strips of cocoanut, plantains,
bananas short and fat, sickly little apples, dwarf
peaches, small wild grapes, oranges green in color,
potatoes often no larger than marbles, as if the possessor could not wait until they grew up before
digging them; cactus leaves, the spines shaved off,
cut up into tiny squares to serve as food; bundles
of larger cactus spines brought in by hobbling old
women or on dismal asses and sold as fuel, *aguacates*,
known to us as " alligator pears " and tasting to the
uninitiated like axle-grease; pomegranates, pecans,
cheeses flat and white, every species of basket and
earthen jar from two-inch size up, turnips, some cut
in two for those who could not afford a whole one;
onions, flat slabs of brown, muddy-looking soap, rice,
every species of frijole or bean, shelled corn for tortillas, tomatoes — *tomate coloradito*, though many
were tiny and green as if also prematurely gathered
— peppers red and green, green-corn with most of
the kernels blue, lettuce, radishes, cucumbers, carrots,
cabbages, melons of every size except large, string-
beans, six-inch cones of the muddiest of sugar, the
first rough product of the crushers wound in swamp
grass and which prospective purchasers handled
over and over, testing them now and then by biting
off a small corner, though there was no apparent
difference; sausages with links of marble size, every-

thing in the way of meat, tossed about in the dirt, swarming with flies, handled, smelled, cut into tiny bits for purchasers; even strips of intestines, the jaw-bone of a sheep with barely the smell of meat on it; all had value to this gaunt community, nothing was too green, or old, or rotten to be offered for sale. Chickens with legs tied lay on the ground or were carried about from day to day until purchasers of such expensive luxuries appeared. There were many men with a little glass box full of squares of sweets like "fudge," selling at a half-cent each; every possible odd and end of the shops was there; old women humped over their meager wares, smoking cigarettes, offered for sale the scraps of calico left over from the cutting of a gown, six-inch triangles of no fathomable use to purchasers. There were entire blocks selling only long strips of leather for the making of sandals. Many a vendor had all the earmarks of leprosy. There were easily five thousand of them, besides another market on the other side of the town, for this poverty-stricken city of some fifty thousand inhabitants. The swarming stretched a half mile away in many a radiating street, and scores whose entire stock could not be worth fifteen cents sat all day without selling more than half of it. An old woman stopped to pick up four grains of corn and greedily tucked them away in the rags that covered her emaciated frame. Now and then a better-dressed *potosino* passed,

The former home, in Dolores Hidalgo, of the Mexican "Father of his Country"

Rancho del Capulín, where I ended the first day of tramping in Mexico

making purchases, a peon, male or female, slinking along behind with a basket; for it is a horrible breach of etiquette for a ten-dollar-a-month Mexican to be publicly seen carrying anything.

One wondered why there was not general suicide in such a community of unmitigated misery. Why did they not spring upon me and snatch the purse I displayed or die in the attempt? How did they resist eating up their own wares? It seemed strange that these sunken-chested, hobbling, halt, shuffling, shivering, starved creatures should still fight on for life. Why did they not suddenly rise and sack the city? No wonder those are ripe for revolution whose condition cannot be made worse.

Policemen in sandals and dark-blue shoddy cap and cloak looked little less miserable than the peons. All about the covered market were peon restaurants, a ragged strip of canvas as roof, under it an ancient wooden table and two benches. Unwashed Indian women cooked in several open earthen bowls the favorite Mexican dishes,— *frijoles* (a stew of brown beans), chile con carne, rice, stews of stray scraps of meat and the leavings of the butcher-shops. These were dished up in brown glazed jars and eaten with strips of tortilla folded between the fingers, as the Arab eats with *gkebis*. Indeed there were many things reminiscent of the markets and streets of Damascus, more customs similar to those of the Moor than the Spaniard could have brought over,

and the brown, wrinkled old women much resembled
those of Palestine, though their noses were flatter
and their features heavier.

Yet it was a good-natured crowd. In all my
wandering in it I heard not an unpleasant word, not
a jest at my expense, almost no evidence of anti-
foreign feeling, which seems not indigenous to the
peon, but implanted in him by those of ulterior
motives. Nor did they once ask alms or attempt
to push misery forward. The least charitable
would be strongly tempted to succor any one of the
throng individually, but here a hundred dollars in
American money divided into Mexican centavos
would hardly go round. Here and there were pulquerías full of besotted, shouting men — and who
would not drink to drown such misery?

There was not a male of any species but had his
colored blanket, red, purple, Indian-yellow, generally with two black stripes, the poorer with a strip
of old carpet. These they wound about their
bodies, folding them across the chest, the arms
hugged together inside in such a way as to bring
a corner across the mouth and nose, leaving their
pipe-stem legs below, and wandered thus dismally
about in the frequent spurts of cold rain. Now and
then a lowest of the low passed in the cast-off remnants of " European " clothes, which were evidently
considered far inferior to peon garb, however bedraggled. Bare or sandaled feet seemed impervious

to cold, again like the Arab, as was also this fear of the raw air and half covering of the face that gave a Mohammedan touch, especially to the women. To me the atmosphere was no different than late October in the States. The peons evidently never shaved, though there were many miserable little barber-shops. On the farther outskirts of the hawkers were long rows of shanties, shacks made of everything under the sun, flattened tin cans, scraps of rubbish, two sticks holding up a couple of ragged bags under which huddled old women with scraps of cactus and bundles of tiny fagots.

Scattered through the throng were several " readers." One half-Indian woman I passed many times was reading incessantly, with the speed of a Frenchman, from printed strips of cheap colored paper which she offered for sale at a cent each. They were political in nature, often in verse, insulting in treatment, and mixed with a crass obscenity at which the dismal multitude laughed bestially. Three musicians, one with a rude harp, a boy striking a triangle steel, sang mournful dirges similar to those of Andalusia. The peons listened to both music and reading motionless, with expressionless faces, with never a " move on " from the policeman, who seemed the least obstrusive of mortals.

San Luís Potosí has many large rich churches, misery and pseudo-religion being common joint-legacies of Spanish rule. Small chance these crea-

tures would have of feeling at home in a place so
different from their earthly surroundings as the
Christian heaven.   The thump of church bells, some
with the voice of battered old tin pans, broke out
frequently.   Now and then one of these dregs of
humanity crept into church for a nap, but the huge
edifices showed no other sign of usefulness.   On the
whole there was little appearance of " religion."   A
few women were seen in the churches, a book-seller
sold no novels and little literature but " mucho de
religión," but the great majority gave no outward
sign of belonging to any faith.   Priests were not
often seen in the streets.   Mexican law forbids them
to wear a distinctive costume, hence they dressed in
black derbies, Episcopal neckbands, and black capes
to the ankles.   Not distinctive indeed!   No one
could have guessed what they were!   One might have
fancied them prize-fighters on the way from train-
ing quarters to bathroom.

There is comparative splendor also in San Luís, as
one may see by peeps into the lighted houses at night,
but it is shut in tight as if fearful of the poor breaking in.   As in so many Spanish countries, wealth
shrinks out of sight and misery openly parades
itself.

Out across the railroad, where hundreds of ragged
boys were riding freight cars back and forth in front
of the station, the land lay flat as a table, some
cactus here and there, but apparently fertile, with

neither sod to break nor clearing necessary. Yet nowhere, even on the edge of the starving city, was there a sign of cultivation. We of the North were perhaps kinder to the Indian in killing him off.

CHAPTER II

HEAVY weather still hung over the land to the southward. Indian corn, dry and shriveled, was sometimes shocked as in the States. The first field of maguey appeared, planted in long rows, barely a foot high, but due in a year or two to produce pulque, the Mexican scourge, because of its cheapness, stupefying the poorer classes. When fresh, it is said to be beneficial in kidney troubles and other ailments, but soon becomes over fermented in the pulquerías of the cities and more harmful than a stronger liquor.

Within the car was an American of fifty, thin and drawn, with huddled shoulders, who had been beaten by rebel forces in Zacatecas and robbed of his worldly wealth of $13,000 hidden in vain in his socks. Numbers of United States box-cars jolted across the country end to end with Mexican; the " B. & O." behind the " Norte de Méjico," the " N. Y. C.," followed by the " Central Mejicano." Long broad stretches of plain, with cactus and mesquite, spread to low mountains blue with cold morning mist, all but

their base hung with fog. Beyond Jesús María,
which is a sample of the station names, peons lived in
bedraggled tents along the way, and the corn was
even drier. The world seemed threatening to dry up
entirely. At Cartagena there began veritable forests of cactus trees, and a wild scrub resembling the
olive. Thousands of *tunas*, the red fruit of the
cactus, dotted the ground along the way. The sun
sizzled its way through the heavy sky as we climbed
the flank of a rocky range, the vast half forested
plain to the east sinking lower and lower as we rose.
Then came broken country with many muddy streams.
It was the altitude perhaps that caused the patent
feeling of exhilaration, as much as the near prospect
of taking again to the open road.

As the " garrotero " (" twister," or " choker " as
the brakeman is called in Mexico) announced Dolores
Hidalgo, I slipped four cartridges into my automatic. The roadways of Mexico offered unknown
possibilities. A six-foot street-car drawn — when
at all — by mules, stood at the station, but I struck
off across the rolling country by a footpath that
probably led to the invisible town. A half-mile lay
behind me before I met the first man. He was riding
an ass, but when I gave him " Buenos días," he replied with a whining: " Una limosnita! A little
alms, for the love of God." He wore a rosary about
his neck and a huge cross on his chest. When I ig-
nored his plea he rode on mumbling. The savage

bellow of a bull not far off suggested a new possible danger on the road in this unfenced and almost tree-less country.   More men passed on asses, mules, and horses, but none afoot.   Finally over the brown rise appeared Dolores Hidalgo; two enormous churches and an otherwise small town in a tree-touched valley. The central plaza, with many trees and hedges trimmed in the form of animals, had in its center the statue of the priest Hidalgo y Costilla, the "father of Mexican independence."   A block away, packed with pictures and wreathes and with much of the old furniture as he left it, was the house in which he had lived before he started the activities that ended in the loss of his head.

Well fortified at the excellent hotel, I struck out past the patriot priest's house over an arched bridge into the open country.   As in any unknown land, the beginning of tramping was not without a certain mild misgiving.   The "road" was only a trail and soon lost itself.   A boy speaking good Spanish walked a long mile to set me right, and valued his services at a *centavo*.   A half-cent seemed to be the fixed fee for anything among these country people. A peon carrying a load of deep-green alfalfa de-manded as much for the privilege of photographing him when he was "not dressed up."   He showed no sign whatever of gratitude when I doubled it and added a cigarette.

The bright sun had now turned the day to early

View of the city of Guanajuato

June. The so-called road was a well-trodden sandy path between high cactus hedges over rolling country. An hour out, the last look back on Dolores Hidalgo showed also mile upon mile of rolling plain to far, far blue sierras, all in all perhaps a hundred square miles visible. There were many travelers, chiefly on foot and carrying bundles on their heads. The greeting of these was " Adiós," while the better-to-do class on horse or mule back used the customary " Buenas tardes! " Thirst grew, but though the country was broken, with many wash-outs cutting deep across the trail, the streams were all muddy. Now and then a tuna on the cactus hedges was red ripe enough to be worth picking and, though full of seeds, was at least wet. It was harder to handle than a porcupine, and commonly left the fingers full of spines. Two men passed, offering *dulces*, a species of native candy, for sale. I declined. " Muy bien, give us a cigarette." I declined again, being low in stock. " Very well, adiós, señor," they replied in the apathetic way of their race, as if it were quite as satisfactory to them to get nothing as what they asked.

The Rancho del Capulín, where night overtook me, was a hamlet of eight or ten houses, some mere stacks of thatch, out of the smoky doorway of which, three feet high, peered the half-naked inmates; others of adobe, large bricks of mud and chopped straw, which could be picked to pieces with the fingers.

From one of the kennels a woman called out to know if I would eat. I asked if she could give lodging also and she referred me to her husband inside. I stopped to peer in through the doorway and he answered there was not room enough as it was, which was evident to the slowest-witted, for the family of six or eight of all ages, more or less dressed, lying and squatted about the earth floor dipping their fingers into bowls of steaming food, left not a square foot unoccupied. He advised me to go " beg license " of the " señora " of the house farther on, a low adobe building with wooden doors.

" There is nothing but the place opposite," she answered.

This was a sort of mud cave, man-made and doorless, the uneven earth floor covered with excrement, human and otherwise. I returned to peer into the mat-roofed yard with piles of corn-stalks and un-threshed beans, and met the man of the house just arriving with his labor-worn burros. He was a sinewy peasant of about fifty, dressed like all country peons in shirt and tight trousers of thinnest white cotton, showing his brown skin here and there. As he hesitated to give me answer, the wife made frantic signs to him from behind the door, of which the cracks were inches wide. He caught the hint and replied to my request for lodging:

" Only if you pay me three centavos."

Such exorbitance! The regulation price was perhaps one. But I yielded, for it was raining, and entered, to sit down on a heap of unthreshed beans. The woman brought me a mat three feet long, evidently destined to be my bed. I was really in the family barnyard, with no end walls, chickens overhead and the burros beyond. The rain took to dripping through the mat roof, and as I turned back toward the first hut for the promised frijoles and tortillas the woman called to me to say she also could furnish me supper.

The main room of the house was about ten by ten, with mud walls five feet high, a pitched roof of some sort of grass with several holes in it. In the center of the room was a fireplace three feet high and four square, with several steaming glazed pots over a fire of *encinal* fagots. The walls were black with soot of the smoke that partly wandered out of an irregular hole in the farther end of the room. The eight-year-old son of the family was eating corn-stalks with great gusto, tearing off the rind with his teeth and chewing the stalk as others do sugar-cane. I handed him a loaf of potosino bread and he answered a perfunctory " Gracias," but neither he nor any of the family showed any evidence of gratitude as he wolfed it. The man complained that all the corn had dried up for lack of rain. The woman set before me a bowl of " sopita," with tortillas, white cheese, and boiled whole peppers. A penniless peon traveler begged a cigarette and half my morning loaf, and

went out into the night and rain to sleep in the
" chapel," as the mud cave across the way was called.
There several travelers had settled down for the
night. A girl of seventeen or so splashed across
from it to beg " a jar of water for a poor prosti-
tute," apparently announcing her calling merely as
a curious bit of information.

The family took at last to eating and kept it up
a full hour, meanwhile discussing me thoroughly.
Like most untutored races, they fancied I could not
understand their ordinary tones. When they wished
to address me they merely spoke louder. It is remarkable how Spain has imposed her language on
even these wild, illiterate Indians as England has not
even upon her colonies. As the rain continued to
pour, I was to sleep in the kitchen. Drunken peons
were shouting outside and the family seemed much
frightened, keeping absolute silence. The four by
two door with its six-inch cracks was blocked with a
heavy pole, the family retired to the other room, and
I stretched out in the darkness on the unsteady
wooden bench, a foot wide, my head on my knapsack.
I was soon glad of having a sweater, but that failed
to cover my legs, and I slept virtually not at all
through a night at least four months long, punctuated by much howling of dogs.

It was still pitch dark when the " señora " entered,
to spend a long time getting a fire started with wet
fagots. Then she began making atole. Taking

shelled corn from an earthen jar, she sprinkled it in
the hallow of a stone and crushed it with much labor.
This was put into water, strained through a sieve,
then thrown into a kettle of boiling water. It was
much toil for little food. Already she had labored
a full hour. I asked for coffee, and she answered
she had none but would buy some when the " store "
opened. It grew broad daylight before this hap-
pened and I accepted atole. It was hot, but as taste-
less as might be the water from boiled corn-stalks.
There had been much discussion, supposedly unknown
to me, the night before as to how much they dared
charge me. The bill was finally set at twelve centavos (six cents), eight for supper, three for lodging,
and one for breakfast. It was evidently highly exorbitant, for the family expressed to each other their
astonishment that I paid it without protest.

At the very outset there was a knee-deep river to
cross. Then miles of a " gumbo " mud that stuck
like bad habits. My feet at times weighed twenty
pounds each. Wild rocky hillsides alternated with
breathless climbs. Many cattle were scattered far
and wide over the mountains, but there was no cultivation. I passed an occasional *rancho*, villages of
six or seven adobe or thatch huts, with sometimes a
ruined brick chapel. Flowers bloomed thickly, morning glories, geraniums, masses of a dark purple blos-
som. The " road " was either a mud-hole or a sharp
path of jagged rolling stones in a barren, rocky,

tumbled country.   Eleven found me entering another
rancho in a wild valley.   My attempts to buy food
were several times answered with, " Más arribita "—
" A little higher up."   I came at last to the " restaurant."   It was a cobble-stone hut hung on a
sharp hillside, with a hole two feet square opening on
the road.   Two men in gay sarapes, with guns and
belts of huge cartridges, reached it at the same time,
and we squatted together on the ground at an angle
of the wall below the window and ate with much exchange of banter the food poked out to us.   The
two had come that morning from Guanajuato,
whither I was bound, and were headed for Dolores.
It was the first time I had any certain information
as to the distance before me, which had been variously
reported at from five to forty leagues.   We ate two
bowls of frijoles each, and many tortillas and chiles.
One of the men paid the entire bill of twenty-seven
centavos, but accepted ten from me under protest.

Beyond was a great climb along a stony, small
stream up into a blackish, rocky range.   The sun
shone splendidly, also hotly.   Apparently there was
no danger to travelers even in these wild parts.   The
peons I met were astonishingly *in*curious, barely appearing to notice my existence.   Some addressed me
as " jefe " (chief), suggesting the existence of mines
in the vicinity.   If I drew them into conversation
they answered merely in monosyllables: " Sí, señor."
" No, jefe."   Not a word of Indian dialect had I

heard since entering the country.   Two hours above
the restaurant a vast prospect of winding, tumbled,
rocky valley and mountain piled upon mountain beyond opened out.   From the summit, surely nine
thousand feet up, began the rocky descent to the
town of Santa Rosa, broken by short climbs and
troublesome with rocks.   I overtook many donkeys
loaded with crates of cactus fruit, railroad ties, and
the like, and finally at three came out in sight of the
famous mining city of Guanajuato.

It would take the pen of a master to paint the
blue labyrinth of mountains heaped up on all sides
and beyond the long, winding city in the narrow
gorge far below, up out of which came with each
puff of wind the muffled sound of stamp-mills and
smelters.   As I sat, the howling of three drunken
peons drifted up from the road below.   When they
reached me, one of them, past forty, thrust his unwashed, pulque-perfumed face into mine and demanded a cigarette.   When I declined, he continued
to beg in a threatening manner.   Meanwhile the
drunkest of the three, a youth of perhaps seventeen,
large and muscular, an evil gleam in his eye, edged
his way up to me with one arm behind him and added
his demands to that of the other.   I suddenly pulled
the hidden hand into sight and found in it a sharp
broken piece of rock weighing some ten pounds.
Having knocked this out of his grasp, I laid my automatic across my knees and the more sober pair

dragged the belligerent youth on up the mountain trail.

For an hour the way wound down by steep, horribly cobbled descents, then between mud and stone huts, and finally down a more level and wider cobbled street along which were the rails of a mule tramway. The narrow city wound for miles along the bottom of a deep gully, gay everywhere with perennial flowers. The main avenue ran like a stream along the bottom, and he who lost himself in the stair-like side streets had only to follow downward to find it again as surely as a tributary its main river. Masses of rocky mountains were piled up on all sides.

The climate of Guanajuato is unsurpassed. Brilliant sunshine flooded days like our early June, in which one must hurry to sweat in the noon time, while two blankets made comfortable covering at night. This is true of not only one season but the year around, during which the thermometer does not vary ten degrees. July is coldest and a fireplace not uncomfortable in the evening. An American resident who went home to one of the States bordering on Canada for his vacation sat wiping the sweat out of his eyes there, when one of his untraveled countrymen observed:

" You must feel very much at home in this heat after nine years in Mexico."

Whereupon the sufferer arose in disgust, packed his bag, and sped south to mosquitoless coolness.

Fellow-roadsters in Mexico

Some of the pigeon-holes of Guanajuato's cemetery

The evening air is indescribable; all nature's changes of striking beauty; and the setting sun throwing its last rays on the Bufa, the salient points of that and the other peaks purple with light, with the valleys in deep shadow, is a sight worth tramping far to see.

I drifted down along the gully next morning, following the main street, which changed direction every few yards, "paved" with three-inch cobbles, the sidewalks two feet wide, leaving one pedestrian to jump off it each time two met. A diminutive streetcar drawn by mules with jingling bells passed now and then. Peons swarmed here also, but there was by no means the abject poverty of San Luís Potosí, and Americans seemed in considerable favor, as their mines in the vicinity give the town its livelihood. I was seeking the famous old "Alóndiga," but the policeman I asked began looking at the names of the shops along the way as if he fancied it some tobacco booth. I tried again by designating it as "la cárrel." He still shook his head sadly. But when I described it as the place where Father Hidalgo's head hung on a hook for thirteen years, a great light broke suddenly upon him and he at once abandoned his beat and led me several blocks, refusing to be shaken off. What I first took for extreme courtesy, however, turned out to be merely the quest of tips, an activity in which the police of most Mexican cities are scarcely outdone by the waiters along Broadway.

The ancient building was outwardly plain and nearly square, more massive than the rest of the city. High up on each of its corners under the rusted hooks were the names of the four early opponents to Spanish rule whose heads had once hung there. Inside the corridor stood the statue of the peon who is said to have reached and fired the building under cover of the huge slab of stone on his back. When I had waited a while in the anteroom, the *jefe político*, the supreme commander of the city appointed by the governor of the State, appeared, the entire roomful of officials and visitors dropping their cigarettes and rising to greet him with bared heads. He gave me permission to enter, and the *presidente*, a podgy second jailor, took me in charge as the iron door opened to let me in. The walls once red with the blood of Spaniards slaughtered by the forces of the priest of Dolores had lost that tint in the century since passed, and were smeared with nothing more startling than a certain lack of cleanliness. The immense, three-story, stone building of colonial days enclosed a vast patio in which prisoners seemed to enjoy complete freedom, lying about the yard in the brilliant sunshine, playing cards, or washing themselves and their scanty clothing in the huge stone fountain in the center. The so-called cells in which they were shut up in groups during the night were large chambers that once housed the colonial government. By day many of them work at weaving hats, baskets, brushes, and the like, to sell for their own benefit, thus being able to order food from outside and avoid the mess brought in barrels at two and seven of each afternoon for those dependent on government rations. Now and then a wife or feminine friend of one of the prisoners appeared at the grating with a basket of food. Several of the inmates were called one by one to the crack of an iron door in the wall to hear the sentence the judge had chosen to impose upon them in the quiet of his own home; for public jury trial is not customary in Spanish America.

In the fine gallery around the patio, in the second-story, we were joined by an American from Colorado, charged with killing a Mexican, but who seemed little worried with his present condition or doubtful of his ultimate release. From the flat roof, large enough for a school playground, there spread out a splendid view of all the city and its surrounding mountains. There were, all told, some five hundred prisoners. A room opening on the patio served as a school for convicts, where a man well advanced in years, bewhiskered and of a decidedly pedagogical cast of countenance in spite of his part Indian blood, sat on his back, peering dreamily through his glasses at the seventy or more pupils, chiefly between the ages of fifteen and twenty, who drowsed before him.

There is a no less fine view from the hill behind, on which sits the Panteón, or city cemetery. It is a rectangular place enclosing perhaps three acres, and,

as all Guanajuato has been buried here for centuries,
considerably crowded. For this reason and from
inherited Spanish custom, bodies are seldom buried,
but are pigeonholed away in the deep nitches two
feet square into what from the outside looks to be
merely the enclosing wall. Here, in more exact order than prevails in life, the dead of Guanajuato are
filed in series, each designated by a number. Series
six was new and not yet half occupied. A funeral
ends by thrusting the coffin into its appointed pigeon-
hole, which the Indian employees brick up and face
with cement, in which while still soft the name of the
defunct and other information is commonly rudely
scratched with a stick, often with amateur spelling.
Here and there is one in English: —" My Father's
Servant — H. B." Some have marble headpieces
with engraved names, and perhaps a third of the
nitches bear the information " En Perpetuidad," in-
dicating that the rent has been paid up until judgment day. The majority of the corpses, however,
are dragged out after one to five years and dumped
in the common bone-yard, as in all Spanish-speaking
countries. The Indian attendants were even then
opening several in an older series and tossing skulls
and bones about amid facetious banter. The lower
four rows can be reached readily, but not a few suffer the pain of being " skied," where only those who
chance to glance upward will notice them.

There were some graves in the ground, evidently

of the poorer Indian classes. Several had been newly
dug, unearthing former occupants, and a grinning
skull sat awry on a heap of earth amid a few thigh
bones and scattered ribs, all trodden under sandaled
foot-prints. In one hole lay the thick black hair of
what had once been a peon, as intact as any actor's
wig. There is some property in the soil of Guanajuato's Panteón that preserves bodies buried in the
ground without coffins, so that its " mummies " have
become famous. The director attended me in person
and, crossing the enclosure, opened a door in the
ground near the fourth series of nitches, where we
descended a little circular iron stairway. This
opened on a high vaulted corridor, six feet wide and
thirty long. Along this, behind glass doors, stood
some hundred more or less complete bodies shrouded
in sheets. They retained, or had been arranged, in
the same form they had presented in life — peon carriers bent as if still under a heavy burden, old market
women in the act of haggling, *arrieros* plodding behind their imaginary burros. Some had their mouths
wide open, as if they had been buried alive and had
died shouting for release. One fellow stood leaning
against a support, like a man joking with an elbow
on the bar, a glass between his fingers, in the act of
laughing uproariously. Several babies had been
placed upright here and there between the elders.
Most of the corpses wore old dilapidated shoes. In
the farther end of the corridor were stacked thigh-

bones and skulls surely sufficient to fill two box-cars, all facing to the front. I asked how many deaths the collection represented, and the director shrugged his shoulders with an indifferent " Quién sabe? " He who would understand the Mexican, descendant of the Aztecs, must not overlook a certain apathetic indifference to death, and a playful manner with its remains.

Once on earth again, I gave the director a handful of coppers and descended to the town, motley now with market-day. The place swarmed with color; ragged, unwashed males and females squatted on the narrow sidewalks with fruit, sweets, gay blankets and clothing, cast-off shoes and garments, piles of new sandals, spread out in the street before them. Amid the babel of street cries the most persistent was " Agua-miel! "—" Honey water," as the juice of the maguey is called during the twelve hours before fermentation sets in. From twelve to thirty-six hours after its drawing it is intoxicating; from then on, only fit to be thrown away. But the sour stench from each pulquería and many a passing peon proved a forced longevity. Several lay drunk in the streets, but passers-by stepped over or around them with the air of those who do as they hope to be done by. Laughter was rare, the great majority being exceedingly somber in manner. Even their songs are gloomy wails, recalling the Arabs. A few children played at " bull-fight," and here and there two or

three, thanks to the American influence, were engaged in what they fancied was baseball. But for
the most part they were not playful. The young
of both Indians and donkeys are trained early for
the life before them. The shaggy little ass-colts follow their mothers over the cobbled streets and along
mountain trails from birth, and the peon children,
wearing the same huge hat, gay sarape, and tight
breeches as their fathers, or the identical garb of the
mothers, carry their share of the family burden almost from infancy. Everything of whatever size
or shape was carried on the backs or heads of Indians with a supporting strap across the forehead.
A peon passed bearing on his head the corpse of a
baby in an open wooden coffin, scattered with flowers.
Trunks of full size are transported in this way to all
parts of the mountain town, and the Indian who car-
ries the heaviest of them to a mine ten miles away
and two thousand feet above the city over the rocki-
est trails considers himself well paid at thirty cents.
Six peons dog-trotted by from the municipal slaughter-house with a steer on their backs: four carried a
quarter each; one the head and skin; and the last,
heart, stomach, and intestines. Horseshoers worked
in the open streets, using whatever shoes they had
on hand without adjustment, paring down the hoofs
of the animal to fit them. Here and there a policeman on his beat was languidly occupied in making
brushes, like the prisoners of the Alóndiga, and two

I saw whiling away the time making lace! Several
of them tagged my footsteps, eager for some errand.
One feels no great sense of security in a country
whose boyish, uneducated, and ragged guardians of
order cringe around like beggar boys hoping for a
copper.

Saturday is beggar's day, when those who seek
alms more or less surreptitiously during the week are
permitted to pass in procession along the shops,
many of which disburse on this day a fixed sum, as
high as twenty dollars, in copper centavos. Now
and then the mule-cars bowled over a laden ass,
which sat up calmly on its haunches, front feet in the
air, until the obstruction passed. All those of Indian blood were notable for their strong white teeth,
not one of which they seem ever to lose. In the
church a bit higher up several bedraggled women and
pulque-besotted peons knelt before a disgusting rep-
resentation of the Crucifixion. The figure had real
hair, beard, eyebrows, and even eyelashes, with several mortal wounds, barked knees and shins, half the
body smeared with red paint as blood, all in all fit
only for the morgue. Farther on, drowsed the post-
office, noted like all south of the Rio Grande for its
unreliability. Unregistered packages seldom arrive
at their destination, groceries sent from the States to
American residents are at least half eaten en route.
A man of the North unacquainted with the ways of
Mexico sent unregistered a Christmas present of a

A *pulque* street-stand and one of its clients

Prisoners washing in the patio of the former "Alóndiga"

dozen pairs of silk socks. The addressee inquired for them daily for weeks. Finally he wrote for a detailed description of the hectic lost property, and had no difficulty in recognizing at least two pairs as the beak-nosed officials hitched up their trousers to tell him again nothing whatever had come for him. Not long before my arrival a Mexican mail-car had been wrecked, and between the ceiling and the outer wall were found over forty thousand letters postal clerks had opened and thrown there.

I drifted into an " Escuela Gratuita para Niños." The heavy, barn-like door gave entrance to a cobbled corridor, opening on a long schoolroom with two rows of hard wooden benches on which were seated a half hundred little peons aged seven to ten, all raggedly dressed in the identical garb, sandals and all, of their fathers in the streets, their huge straw hats covering one of the walls. The *maestro*, a small, down-trodden-looking Mexican, rushed to the door to bring me down to the front and provide me with a chair. The school had been founded some six months before by a woman of wealth, and offered free instruction to the sons of peons. But the Indians as always were suspicious, and for the most part refused to allow their children to be taught the " witchcraft " of the white man. The teacher asked what class I cared to hear and then himself hastily suggested " cuentitas." The boys were quick at figures, at least in the examples the maestro chose to give them, but he declined to show them off in writing or spelling. Several read aloud, in that mumbled and half-pronounced manner common to Mexico, the only requirement appearing to be speed. Then came a class in " Historia Santa," that is, various of the larger boys arose to spout at full gallop and the distinct enunciation of an " El " train, the biblical account of the creation of the world, the legends of Adam and Eve, Cain and Abel, and Noah's travels with a menagerie, all learned by rote. The entire school then arose and bowed me out.

A visit to a mixed school, presided over by carelessly dressed maidens of uncertain age and the all-knowing glance of those who feel the world and all its knowledge lies concentrated in the hollow of their hands, showed a quite similar method of instruction. On the wall hung a great lithograph depicting in all its dreadful details the alleged horrors of " alcoolismo." Even the teachers rattled off their questions with an atrocious, half-enunciated pronunciation, and he must have been a Spanish scholar indeed who could have caught more than the gist of the recited answers. This indistinctness of enunciation and the Catholic system of learning by rote instead of permitting the development of individual power to think, were as marked even in the *colegio*, corresponding roughly to our high schools. Even there the professor never commanded, " More distinctly!" but he frequently cried, " Faster!"

On the wall of this higher institution was a stern
set of rules, among which some of the most important
were:

" Students must not smoke in the presence of pro-
fessors," though this was but mildly observed, for
when I entered the study room with the director and
his assistant, all of us smoking, the boys, averaging
fifteen years of age, merely held their lighted cigarettes half out of sight behind them until we passed.
Another rule read: " Any student frequenting a
tavern, café chantant, or house of ill-fame may be
expelled." He might run that risk in most schools,
but none but the Latinized races would announce the
fact in plain words on the bulletin-boards. The director complained that the recent revolutions had set
the school far back, as each government left it to the
next to provide for such secondary necessities.

CHAPTER III

IN A MEXICAN MINE

A CLASSMATE of my boyhood was superintendent of the group of mines round about
Guanajuato. From among them we chose " Pingüico " for my temporary employment. The ride to it,
8200 feet above the sea, up along and out of the gully
in which Guanajuato is built, and by steep rocky
trails sometimes beside sheer mountain walls, opens
out many a marvelous vista; but none to compare
with that from the office veranda of the mine itself.
Two thousand feet below lies a plain of Mexico's
great table-land, stretching forty miles or more
across to where it is shut off by an endless range of
mountains, backed by chain after blue chain, each
cutting the sky-line in more jagged, fantastic fashion
than the rest, the farther far beyond Guadalajara
and surely more than a hundred miles distant, where
Mexico falls away into the Pacific. On the left rises
deep-blue into the sky the almost perfect flattened
cone of a lone mountain. Brilliant, yet not hot, sunshine illuminated even the far horizon, and little
cloud-shadows crawled here and there across the

landscape. The rainy season had left on the plain below many shallow lakes that reflected the sun like immense mirrors. From the veranda it seemed quite flat, though in reality by no means so, and one could all but count the windows of Silao, Irapuato, and other towns; the second, though more than twenty miles away, still in the back foreground of the picture. Thread-like, brown trails wound away over the plain and up into the mountains, here and there dotted by travelers crawling ant-like along them a few inches an hour. Take the most perfect day of late May or early June in our North, brush off the clouds, make the air many times fresher and clearer, add October nights, and multiply the sum total by 365, and it is more easily understood why Americans who settle in the Guanajuato region so frequently remain there.

The room I shared with a mine boss was of chilly stone walls and floor, large and square, with a rug, two beds, and the bare necessities. The mine mess, run by a Chinaman, furnished meals much like those of a 25-cent restaurant in Texas, at the rate of $5 a week. No Mexican was permitted to eat with the Americans, not even with the " rough-necks." When the whistle blew at seven next morning, some forty peons, who had straggled one by one in the dawn to huddle up together in their red sarapes among the rocks of the drab hillside, marched past the time-keeper, turning over their blankets at a check counter, and with their lunches, of the size of the round tortilla at the bottom and four to six inches high, in their handkerchiefs, climbed into the six-foot, iron ore-bucket until it was completely roofed with their immense straw hats. Near by those of the second night-shift, homeward bound, halted, to stand one by one on a wooden block with outstretched arms to be carefully searched for stolen ore by a tried and trusted fellow-peon. A pocketful of "high-grade" might be worth several dollars. The American "jefe" sat in the hoisthouse, writing out requisitions for candles, dynamite, and kindred supplies for the "jefecitos," or straw bosses, of the hundred or more peons still lined up before the shaft. With the last batch of these in the bucket, we white men stepped upon the platform below it and dropped suddenly into the black depths of the earth, with now and then a stone easily capable of cracking a skull bounding swiftly with a hollow sound past us back and forth across the shaft.

Not infrequently in the days to come some accident to the hoist-engine above left us to stand an hour or more packed tightly together in our suspended four-foot space in unmitigated darkness. For this and other reasons no peon was ever permitted to ride on the platform with an American. Twelve hundred feet down we stepped out into a winding, rock gallery nearly six feet wide and high, where fourteen natives were loading rock and mud into iron dump-cars and pushing them to a near-by chute. Even at this depth flies were thick. A facetious boss asserted they hatched on the peons. My task here was to " sacar muestras "—" take samples," as it was called in English. From each car as it passed I snatched a handful of mud and small broken rock and thrust it into a sack that later went to the assay office to show what grade of ore the vein was producing.

Once an hour I descended to a hole far beneath by a rope ladder, life depending on a spike driven in the rock above and a secure handhold, for the handful of " pay dirt " two peons were grubbing down out of a lower *veta*, a long narrow alleyway of soft earth and small stones that stretched away into the interior of the mountain between solid walls of rock. No inexperienced man would have supposed this mud worth more than any other. But silver does not come out of the earth in minted dollars.

In the mine the peons wore their hats, a considerable protection against falling rocks, but were otherwise naked but for their sandals and a narrow strip of once white cloth between their legs, held by a string around the waist. Some were well-built, though all were small, and in the concentrated patch of light the play of their muscles through the light-brown skins was fascinating. Working thus naked seemed so much more dangerous; the human form appeared so much more feeble and soft, delving unclothed in the fathomless, rocky earth. Many a man was marked

here and there with long deep scars. It was noticeable how character, habits, dissipation, which show
so plainly in the face, left but little sign on the rest
of the body, which remained for the most part smooth
and unwrinkled.

The peons were more than careless. All day long
dynamite was tossed carelessly back and forth about
me. A man broke up three or four sticks of it at a
time, wrapped them in paper, and beat the mass into
the form of a ball on a rock at my feet. Miners
grow so accustomed to this that they note it, if at
all, with complete indifference, often working and
serenely smoking seated on several hundred pounds
of explosives. One peon of forty in this gang had
lost his entire left arm in a recent explosion, yet he
handled the dangerous stuff as carelessly as ever.
Several others were mutilated in lesser degrees.
They depend on charms and prayers to their favorite saint rather than on their own precautions.
Every few minutes the day through came the cry:
"'Stá pegado!" that sent us skurrying a few feet
away until a dull, deafening explosion brought down
a new section of the vein. Not long before, there had
been a cave-in just beyond where we were working,
and the several men imprisoned there had not been
rescued, so that now and then a skull and portions
of skeleton came down with the rock. The peons had
first balked at this, but the superintendent had told
them the bones were merely strange shapes of ore,

Drilling with compressed-air drills in a mine "heading"

As each car passed I snatched a sample of its ore

ordered them to break up the skulls and throw
them in with the rest, and threatened to discharge and
blackball any man who talked of the matter.

By law a Mexican injured in the mine could not
be treated on the spot, but must be first carried to
Guanajuato — often dying on the way — to be examined by the police and then brought back to the
mine hospital. Small hurts were of slight importance to the peons. During my first hour below, a
muddy rock fell down the front of a laborer, scrap-
ing the skin off his nose, deeply scratching his chest
and thighs, and causing his toes to bleed, but he
merely swore a few round oaths and continued his
work. The hospital doctors asserted that the peon
has not more than one fourth the physical sensitive-
ness of civilized persons. Many a one allowed a
finger to be amputated without a word, and as chloro-
form is expensive the surgeon often replaced it with
a long draught of *mescal* or *tequila*, the native
whiskies.

Outwardly the peons were very deferential to white
men. I could rarely get a sentence from them,
though they chattered much among themselves, with
a constant sprinkling of obscenity. They had a complete language of whistles by which they warned each
other of an approaching " jefe," exchanged varied
information, and even entered into discussion of the
alleged characteristics of their superiors in their
very presence without being understood by the un-

initiated. Frequently, too, amid the rumble of the
" veta madre " pouring down her treasures, some former Broadway favorite that had found its way gradually to the theater of Guanajuato sounded weirdly
through the gallery, as it was whistled by some naked
peon behind a loaded car. A man speaking only the
pure Castilian would have had some difficulty in un-
derstanding many of the mine terms. Many Indian
words had crept into the common language, such as
" chiquihuite " for basket.

Some seventy-five cars passed me during the morning. Under supervision the peons worked at moderately good speed; indeed, they compared rather fa-
vorably with the rough American laborers with whom
I had recently toiled in railroad gangs, in a stone-
quarry of Oklahoma, and the cotton-fields of Texas.
The endurance of these fellows living on corn and
beans is remarkable; they were as superior to the
Oriental coolie as their wages to the latter's eight or
ten cents a day. In this case, as the world over, the
workmen earned about what he was paid, or rather
succeeded in keeping his capacity down to the wages
paid him. Many galleries of the mine were " worked
on contract," and almost all gangs had their self-
chosen leader. A peon with a bit more standing in
the community than his fellows, wearing something
or other to suggest his authority and higher place in
the world — such perhaps as the pink shirt the
haughty " jefecito " beside me sported — appeared

with twelve or more men ready for work and was given a section and paid enough to give his men from fifty to eighty cents a day each and have something over a dollar left for himself. Miners' wages vary much throughout Mexico, from twelve dollars a month to two a day in places no insuperable distances apart. Conditions also differ greatly, according to my experienced compatriots. The striking and booting of the workmen, common in some mines, was never permitted in " Pingüico." In Pachuca, for example, this was said to be the universal practice; while in the mines of Chihuahua it would have been as dangerous as to do the same thing to a stick of dynamite. Here the peon's manner was little short of obsequious outwardly, yet one had the feeling that in crowds they were capable of making trouble and those who had fallen upon " gringoes " in the region had despatched their victims thoroughly, leaving them mutilated and robbed even of their clothing. The charming part of it all was one could never know which of these slinking fellows was a bandit by avocation and saving up his unvented anger for the boss who ordered him about at his labors.

It felt pleasant, indeed, to bask in the sun a half hour after dinner before descending again. Toward five I tied and tagged the sacks of samples and followed them, on peon backs, to the shaft and to the world above with its hot and cold shower-bath, and the Chinaman's promise, thanks to the proximity of

Irapuato, of " stlaybelly pie." Though the American force numbered several of those fruitless in-
dividuals that drift in and out of all mining communi-
ties, it was on the whole of rather high caliber.   Besides " Sully the Pug," a mere human animal, hairy
and muscular as a bear, and two " Texicans," as
those born in the States of some Mexican blood and
generally a touch of foreign accent are called, there
were two engineers who lived with their " chinitas,"
or illiterate *mestizo* Mexican wives and broods of
peon children down in the valley below the dump-
heap.   Caste lines were not lacking even among the
Americans in the " camp," as these call Guanajuato
and its mining environs.   More than one complained
that those who married Mexican girls of unsullied
character and even education were rated " squaw-
men " and more or less ostracized by their fellow
countrymen, and especially country-women, while
the man who " picked up an old rounder from the
States " was looked upon as an equal.   The speech
of all Mexico is slovenly from the Castilian point of
view.   Still more so was that of both the peon and
the Americans, who copied the untutored tongue of
the former, often ignorant of its faults, and generally not in the least anxious to improve, nor indeed
to get any other advantage from the country except
the gold and silver they could dig out of it.   Laborers and bosses commonly used " pierra " for piedra ;
" sa' pa' fuera " for to leave the mine, " croquesí "

Working a "heading" by hand

for I believe so, commonly ignorant even of the fact
that this is not a single word.   In the mess-hall were
heard strange mixtures of the two languages, as
when a man rising to answer some call shouted over
his   shoulder: "Juan,   deja   mi   pie   alone!"
Thanks to much peon intercourse, almost all the
Americans had an unconsciously patronizing air even
to their fellows, as many a pedagogue comes to address all the world in the tone of the schoolroom.
The Mexican, like the Spaniard, never laughs at the
most atrocious attempts at his tongue by foreigners,
and even the peons were often extremely quick-witted
in catching the idea from a few mispronounced words.
"The man with the hair ——," I said one day, in
describing a workman I wished summoned; and not
for the moment recalling the Castilian for curly, I
twirled my fingers in the air.

"Chino!" cried at least a half-dozen peons in the
same breath.

Small wonder the Mexican considers the " gringo "
rude.   An American boss would send a peon to fetch
his key or cigarettes, or on some equally important
errand; the workman would run all the way up hill
and down again in the rarified air, removing his hat
as he handed over the desired article, and the average
man from the States would not so much as grunt his
thanks.

The engineers on whom our lives depended as often
as we descended into or mounted from the mine, had

concocted and posted in the engine-room the following " ten commandments ":

" NOTICE TO VISITORS AND OTHERS

" ARTICLE 1. Be seated on the platform. It is too large for the engineer anyway.

" ART. 2. Spit on the floor. We like to clean up after you.

" ART. 3. Talk to the engineer while he is running. There is no responsibility to his job.

" ART. 4. If the engineer does not know his business, please tell him. He will appreciate it.

" ART. 5. Ask him as many questions as you like. He is paid to answer them.

" ART. 6. Please handle all the bright work. We have nothing to do but clean it.

" ART. 7. Don't spit on the ceiling. We have lost the ladder.

" ART. 8. Should the engineer look angry don't pay any attention to him. He is harmless.

" ART. 9. If you have no cigarettes take his. They grow in his garden.

" ART. 10. If he is not entertaining, report him to the superintendent and he will be fired at once."

On the second day the scene of my operations was changed to the eighth level, a hundred feet below that of the first. It was a long gallery winding away through the mountain, and connecting a mile beyond with another shaft opening on another hill, so that the heavy air was tempered by a constant mild breeze.

Side shafts just large enough for the ore-cars to pass, pierced far back into the mountain at frequent intervals. Back in these it was furnace hot. From them the day-gang took out 115 car-loads, though the chute was blocked now and then by huge rocks that must be " shot " by a small charge of dynamite stuck on them, a new way of " shooting the chutes " that was like striking the ear-drums with a club.

The peons placed in each gallery either a cross or a lithograph of the Virgin in a shrine made of a dynamite-box, and kept at least one candle always burning before it. In the morning it was a common sight to see several appear with a bunch of fresh-picked flowers to set up before the image. Most of the men wore a rosary or charm about the neck, which they did not remove even when working naked, and all crossed themselves each time they entered the mine. Not a few chanted prayers while the cage was descending. As often as they passed the gallery-shrine, they left off for an instant the vilest oaths, in which several boys from twelve to fourteen ex-celled, to snatch off their hats to the Virgin, then in-stantly took up their cursing again. Whenever I left the mine they begged the half-candle I had left, and set it up with the rest. Yet they had none of the touchiness of the Hindu about their superstitions, and showed no resentment whatever even when a " gringo " stopped to light his cigarette at their im-provised " altars."

Trusted miners hired to search the others for stolen ore as they leave the shaft were sometimes waylaid on the journey home and beaten almost or quite to death. Once given a position of authority, they were harsher with their own kind than were the white men. The scarred and seared old " Pingüico " searcher, who stood at his block three times each twenty-four hours, had already killed three men who thus attacked him. Under no provocation whatever would the peons fight underground, but lay for their enemies only outside. A shift-boss in a neighboring mine remained seven weeks below, having his food sent down to him, and continued to work daily with miners who had sworn to kill him once they caught him on earth. One of our engineers had long been accustomed at another mine to hand his revolver to the searcher when the shift appeared and to arm himself with a heavy club. One day the searcher gave the superintendent a " tip," and when the hundred or more were lined up they were suddenly commanded to take off their *borrachas*. A gasp of dismay sounded, but all hastily snatched off their sandals and something like a bushel of high-grade ore in thin strips lay scattered on the ground. But a few mornings later the searcher was found dead half way between the mine and his home.

Some of the mines round about Guanajuato were in a most chaotic state, especially those of individual ownership. The equipment was often so poor that

Peon miners being searched for stolen ore as they leave the mine

Bricks of gold and silver ready for shipment. Each is worth something like $1250

fatal accidents were common, deaths even resulting from rocks falling down the shafts. Among our engineers was one who had recently come from a mine where during two weeks' employment he pulled out from one to four corpses daily, until " it got so monotonous " he resigned. In that same mine it was customary to lock in each shift until the relieving one arrived, and many worked four or five shifts, thirty-two to forty hours without a moment of rest, swallowing a bit of food now and then with a sledge in one hand. " High-graders," as ore-thieves are called, were numerous. The near-by " Sirena " mine was reputed to have in its personnel more men who lived by stealing ore than honest workmen. There ran the story of a new boss in a mine so near ours that we could hear its blasting from our eighth level, long dull thuds that seemed to run through the mountain like a shudder through a human body, who was making his first underground inspection when his light suddenly went out and he felt the cold barrel of a revolver against his temple. A peon voice sounded in the darkness close to his ear :

" No te muevas, hijo de ——, si quieres vivir ! "

Another light was struck and he made out some twenty peons, each with a sack of " high-grade," and was warned to take his leave on the double-quick and not to look around on penalty of a worse fate than that of Lot's wife.

Bandit gangs were known to live in out-of-the-way

corners of several mines, bringing their blankets and tortillas with them and making a business of stealing ore.   Not even the most experienced mining engineer could more quickly recognize " pay dirt " than the peon population of Guanajuato vicinity.

Though he is obsequious enough under ordinary circumstances, the mine peon often has a deep-rooted hatred of the American, which vents itself chiefly in cold silence, unless opportunity makes some more effective way possible.   Next on his black-list comes the Spaniard, who is reputed a heartless usurer who long enjoyed protection under Diaz. Third, perhaps, come the priests, though these are endured as a necessary evil, as we endure a bad government.   The padre of Calderón drifted up to the mine one day to pay his respects and drink the mine health in good Scotch whisky.   Gradually he brought the conversation around to the question of disobedience among the peons, and summed up his advice to the Americans in a vehement explosion:

" Fine them!   Fine them often, and much!

" Of course," he added, as he prepared to leave, " you know that by the laws of Mexico and the *Santa Iglesia* all such fines go to the church."

Intercourse between the mine officials and native authorities was almost always sure to make it worth while to linger in the vicinity.   My disrespectful fellow countrymen were much given to mix in with the most courteous Spanish forms of speech asides in English which it was well the pompous official natives did not understand. I reached the office one day to find the chief of police just arrived to collect for his services in guarding the money brought out on pay-day.

"Ah, señor mío," cried the superintendent, "Y cómo está usted? La familia buena? Y los hijos — I'll slip the old geaser his six bones and let him be on his way — Oh, sí, señor. Cómo no? Con muchísimo gusto — and there goes six of our good bucks and four bits and — Pues adiós, muy señor mío! Vaya bien! — If only you break your worthless old neck on the way home — Adiós pues!"

After the shower-bath it was as much worth while to stroll up over the ridge back of the camp and watch the night settle down over this upper-story world. Only on the coast of Cochinchina have I seen sunsets to equal those in this altitude. Each one was different. To-night it stretched entirely across the saw-toothed summits of the western hills in a narrow, pinkish-red streak; to-morrow the play of colors on mountains and clouds shot blood-red, fading to saffron yellow growing an ever-thicker gray down to the horizon, with the unrivaled blue of the sky overhead, all shifting and changing with every moment, would be hopelessly beyond the power of words. Often rain was falling in a spot or two far to the west, and there the clouds were jet black. In one place well above the horizon was perhaps a

brilliant pinkish patch of reflected sun, and everything else an immensity of clouded sky running from
Confederate gray above to a blackish-blue that
blended with range upon range to the uttermost distance.

There was always a peculiar stillness over all
the scene. Groups of sandaled mine peons wound
noiselessly away, a few rods apart, along undulating
trails, the red of their sarapes and the yellow of their
immense hats giving the predominating hue. In
the vast landscape was much green, though more
gray of outcropping rocks. Here and there a lonely
telegraph wire struck off dubiously across the rugged country. Rocks as large as houses hung on the
great hillsides, ready to roll down and destroy at the
slightest movement of the earth, like playthings left
by careless giant children. Along some rocky path
far down in the nearer valley a small horse of the
patient Mexican breed, under its picturesque, huge-
hatted rider, galloped sure-footed up and down steep
faces of rock. Cargadores bent half double, with
a rope across their brows, came straining upward
to the mine. Bands of peons released from their underground labors paused here and there on the way
home to wager cigarettes on which could toss a stone
nearest the next mud puddle. Flocks of goats wandered in the growing dusk about swift rocky mountain flanks. Farther away was a rocky ridge beaten
with narrow, bare, crisscross trails, and beyond, the

old Valenciana mine on the flanks of the jagged range shutting off Dolores Hidalgo, appearing so near in this clear air of the heights that it seemed a man could throw a stone there; yet down in the valley between lay all Guanajuato, the invisible, and none might know how many bandits were sleeping out the day in their lurking-places among the wild, broken valleys and gorges the view embraced. Down in its rock-tumbled valley spread the scattered town of Calderón, and the knell of its tinny old church bells came drifting up across the divide on the sturdy evening breeze, tinged with cold, that seemed to bring the night with it, so silently and coolly did it settle down. The immense plain and farther mountains remained almost visible in the starlight, in the middle distance the lamps of Silao, and near the center of the half-seen picture those of Irapuato, while far away a faint glow in the sky marked the location of the city of Leon.

Excitement burst upon the mess-table one night. Rival politicians were to contend the following Sunday for the governorship of the State, and the " liberal " candidate had assured the peons that he would treble their wages and force the company to give them full pay during illness, and that those who voted for his rival were really casting ballots for " los gringos " who had stolen away their mines. All this was, of course, pure campaign bunco; as a matter of fact the lowest wages in all the mines of Mexico were in those belonging to the then "liberal" President of the republic, and accident pay would have caused these insensible fellows to drop rocks on themselves to enjoy its benefits. For several mornings threatening political posters had appeared on the walls of the company buildings. But this time word came that "liberal" posters had been stuck up in the galleries of the mine itself. The boss sprang to his feet, and without even sending for his revolver went down into the earth. An hour or more later he reappeared with the remnants of the posters. Though the mine was populated with peons and there was not then another American below ground, they watched him tear down the sheets without other movement than to cringe about him, each begging not to be believed guilty. Later a peon was charged with the deed and forever forbidden to work in the mines of the company. The superintendent threatened to discharge any employee who voted for the "liberal" candidate, and, though he could not of course know who did, their dread of punishment no doubt kept many from voting at all.

Work in the mine never ceased. Even as we fell asleep the engine close at hand panted constantly, the mild clangor of the blacksmith-shop continued unbroken, cars of rock were dumped every few minutes under the swarming stars, the mine pulse beat unchanging, and far down beneath our beds hundreds

of naked peons were still tearing incessantly at the
rocky entrails of the earth.

Though the mine throbbed on, I set off on sunny
Sunday morning to walk to town and the weekly
ball game. It was just warm enough for a summer
coat, a breeze blew as at sea, an occasional telephone
pole was singing as with contentment with life in this
perfect climate. Groups of brownish-gray donkeys
with loads on their backs passed me or crawled along
far-away trails, followed by men in tight white
trousers, their striped and gay-colored sarapes about
their bodies and their huge hats atop. Over all was
a Sunday stillness, broken only by the occasional
bark of a distant dog or a cockcrow that was almost
musical as it was borne by on the wind. Everywhere
were mountains piled into the sky. Valenciana,
where so many Spaniards, long since gone to whatever reward awaited them, waxed rich and built a
church now golden brown with age, sat on its slope
across the valley down in which no one would have
guessed huddled a city of some 60,000 inhabitants.
Much nearer and a bit below drowsed the old town
of Calderón, home of many of our peons, a bright
red blanket hung over a stone wall giving a splash
of brilliancy to the vast stretch of grayish, dull-
brown, and thirsty green. The road wound slowly
down and ever down, until the gullies grew warmer as
the rising mountains cut off the breeze and left the

sun in undisputed command. Along the way were
flowers uncountable, chiefly large, white, lily-like
blossoms growing on a bush, then thick patches of
orange-yellow. Horsemen, Mexicans on burros,
peon men, women, and children afoot were legion.
There were no Americans, though I passed one huge
Negro with a great black beard who gave me " Good
morning " from his horse in the tone of a man who
had not met an equal before in some time. At length
appeared the emerald-green patch of the upper
Presa, with its statue of Hidalgo, and the café-au-
lait pond that stores the city's water, and over the
parapet of which hung *guanajuatenses* watching
with wonder the rowboat of the American hospital
doctor, the only water craft the great majority of
them had ever seen.

A natural amphitheater encloses the ball-ground
in which were gathered the wives of Americans, in
snowy white, to watch a game between teams made
up chiefly of " gringoes " of the mines, my one-time
classmate still at short-stop, as in our schoolboy
days, thanks to which no doubt Guanajuato held the
baseball championship of Mexico. Like the English
officials of India, the Americans in high places here
were noticeable for their youth, and at least here on
the ball-ground for their democracy, known to all
by their boyhood nicknames yet held almost in rev-
erence by the Mexican youths that filled in the less
important positions. At the club after the game the

In a natural amphitheater of Guanajuato the American miners of the region gather on Sundays for a game of baseball

Some of the peons under my charge about to leave the mine

champion Mexican player discoursed on the certainty
of ultimate American intervention and expressed his
own attitude with:

"Let it come, for I am not a politician but a
baseball player."

It was election day, and I passed several doorways, among them that of the company stable, in
which a half-dozen old fossils in their most solemn
black garb crouched dreamily over wooden tables
with registers, papers, and ink bottles before them.
Now and then a frightened peon slunk up hat in hand
to find whether they wished him to vote, and how, or
to see if perhaps he had not voted already — by absent treatment. The manager of one of the mines
had come into the office of the jefe político of his district the night before and found the ballots already
made out for the " liberal " candidate. He tore
them up and sent his own men to watch the election,
with the result that there was a strong majority in
that precinct in favor of the candidate more pleasing to the mine owners. The pulquerías and saloons
of the peons had been closed, but not the clubs and
resorts of the white men. In one of these I sat with
the boss, watching him play a game of stud poker.
A dissipated young American, who smoked a cigar
and a cigarette at the same time, was most in evidence, a half Comanche Indian of an utterly im-
passive countenance did the dealing, and fortunes
went up and down amid the incessant rattle of chips

far into the morning. At three the boss broke
away, nine dollars to the good, while the proprietor
of the place ended with an enormous heap of chips
in front of him; another American, making out to
him a check for $90, and calling for his horse, rode
back to his mine to earn it — the shoes of the horse
clanking on the cobbles in the silence of the night
and passing now and then a policeman's lantern set
in the middle of the street, while that official huddled in his white uniform in a dark corner, ostensibly keeping guard.

On another such a day I turned back about dusk
up the gorge on the return to the mine.   The upper
park where the band had played earlier was now
completely deserted.   The road was nearly five miles
long; the trail, sheer up the wild tumble of mountains before me, little more than two.   This was
vaguely reputed dangerous, but I was not inclined
to take the rumor seriously.

Black night fell.   Soon I came upon the vanguard
of the day-shift from " Pingüico," straggling down
the face of the mountain, shouting and whistling to
each other in their peculiar language.   Some carried torches that flashed along the mountain wall
above me and threw long quaint shadows of the tight-
trousered legs.   The grade was more than forty-
five degrees, with much slipping and sliding on unseen rocks.   Two or three groups had passed when
one of the men recognized me and with a " Buenas

noches, jefe!" insisted on giving me the torch he carried, a mine candle with a cloth wrapped around it as a protection in the strong wind. I had soon to cast this away, as it not only threatened to burn my hand but left the eyes unable to pierce the surrounding wall of darkness. In the silence of the night there came to mind the assertion of by no means our most timorous engineer, that he never passed over this trail after dark without carrying his revolver cocked in his hand. My fellow countrymen of the region all wore huge " six-shooters " with a large belt of cartridges always in sight, less for use than the salutary effect of having them visible, in itself a real protection. Conditions in Mexico had led me to go armed for the first time in my travels; or more exactly, to carry one of the " vest pocket automatics " so much in vogue — on advertising pages — in that season. My experienced fellow Americans refused to regard this weapon seriously. One had made the very fitting suggestion that each bullet should bear a tag with the devise, " You 're shot!" An aged " roughneck " of a half-century of Mexican residence had put it succinctly: " Yer travel scheme 's all right; but I 'll be —— —— if I like the gat you carry." However, such as it was, I drew it now and held it ready for whatever it might be called upon to attempt.

A half hour of heavy climbing brought me to the summit, with a strong cool breeze and a splendid

view of the spreading lights of Guanajuato in the
narrow winding gully far below. The trail wound
round a peak and reached the first scattered huts of
Calderón just as a number of shots sounded not far
away. These increased until all the dogs for miles
around took up the hue and cry. The shots multiplied, with much shouting and uproar, soon sound-
ing on both sides and ahead and behind me, while
the whistling language shrilled from every gully and
hillside. Evidently drunken peons were harmlessly
celebrating their Sunday holiday, but the shots
sounded none the less weirdly out of the black night
as I stumbled on over the rocky, tumbled country,
for the only smooth way thereabouts was the Milky
Way faintly seen overhead. Gradually the shooting and shouting drifted behind me and died out as
I surmounted the last knoll and descended to bed.
It was only at breakfast next morning that I learned
I had serenely strolled through a pitched battle between bandits that haunted the recesses of the mountains about Calderón and the town which, led by
its jefe político, had finally won the bout with four
outlaw corpses to its credit. It was my luck not to
have even a bullet-hole through my cap to prove the
story. There were often two or three such battles
a week in the vicinity.

That morning I was given a new job. The boss
led the way, candle in hand, a half mile back through
the bowels of the mountain, winding with the swing-

The easiest way to carry a knapsack—on a peon's back

The ore thieves of Peregrina being led away to prison

ing of the former ore vein. This alone was enough
to get hopelessly lost in, even without its many blind-
alley branches. Now and then we came upon another shaft-opening that seemed a bottomless hole
a few feet in diameter in the solid rock, from far
down which came up the falsetto voices and the
stinking sweat of peons, and the rap, rap of heavy
hammers on iron rock-bars. But we had only
started. Far back in the gallery we took another
hoist and descended some two hundred feet more,
then wound off again through the mountain by more
labyrinthian burrowings in the rock, winding, undulating passages, often so low we must crawl on
hands and knees, with no other light than the flickering candles half-showing shadowy forms of naked,
copper-colored beings; the shadows giving them
often fiendish faces and movements, until we could
easily imagine ourselves in the realms of Dante's
imagination. In time we came to a ladder leading
upward into a narrow dark hole, and when the ladder ended we climbed some forty feet higher on our
bellies up a ledge of rock to another heading, along
which we made our way another hundred yards or
more to where a dozen naked peons were operating
compressed-air drills; then wormed our way like
snakes over the resultant debris to the present end of
the passage where more peons were drilling by hand,
one man holding a bar of iron a few feet long which
another was striking with a five-pound sledge that

luckily never missed its mark. This was indeed working *in* Mexico. It would have been difficult to get farther into it; and a man could not but dully wonder if he would ever get out again.

We were evidently very close to the infernal regions. Here, indeed, would have been a splendid setting for an orthodox hell. Peons whose only garment was the size of a postcard, some even with their hats off, glistened all over their brown bodies as under a shower-bath. In five minutes I had sweat completely through my garments, in ten I could wring water out of my jacket; drops fell regularly at about half-second intervals from the end of my nose and chin. The dripping sweat formed puddles beneath the toilers, the air was so scarce and second-hand every breath was a deep gasp; nowhere a sign of exit, as if we had been walled up in this narrow, low-ceiled, jagged-rock passageway for all time.

My work here was to take samples from the " roof." A grinning peon who called himself " Bruno Básques " (Vásquez) followed me about, holding his hat under the hammer with which I chipped bits of rock from above, back and forth across the top of the tunnel every few feet. The ore ran very high in grade here, the vein being some six feet of whitish rocky substance between sheer walls of ordinary rock. It struck one most forcibly, this strange inquisitiveness of man that had caused him to prowl around inside the earth like a mole, looking for a peculiar kind of soil or stone which no one at first sight could have guessed was of any particular value. The peons, smeared all over with the drippings of candle-grease, worked steadily for all the heat and stuffiness. Indeed, one could not but wonder at the amount of energy they sold for a day's wages; though of course their industry was partly due to my " gringo " presence. We addressed them as inferiors, in the " tu " form and with the generic title " hombre," or, more exactly, in the case of most of the American bosses, " húm-bray." The white man who said " please " to them, or even showed thanks in any way, such as giving them a cigarette, lost caste in their eyes as surely as with a butler one might attempt to treat as a man. I tried it on Bruno, and he almost instantly changed from obsequiousness to near-insolence. When I had put him in his place again, he said he was glad I spoke Spanish, for so many " jefes " had pulled his hair and ears and slapped him in the face because he did not understand their " strange talk." He did not mention this in any spirit of complaint, but merely as a curious fact and one of the many visitations fate sees fit to send those of her children unluckily born peons. His jet black hair was so thick that small stones not only did not hurt his head as they fell from under my hammer, but remained buried in his thatch, so that nearly as many samples were taken from this as from the roof of the passage.

Thus the sweat-dripping days passed, without a hint of what might be going on in the world far above, amid the roar and pounding of air and hand-drills, the noisy falling of masses of rock as these broke it loose, the constant ringing of shovels, the rumble of iron ore-cars on their thread-like rails, cries of " 'stá pegado! " quickly followed by the stunning, ear-splitting dynamite blast, screams of "No vás echar! " as some one passed beneath an opening above, of " Ahora sí! " when he was out of danger; the shrill warning whistling of the peons echoing back and forth through the galleries and labyrinthian side tunnels, as the crunch of shoes along the track announced the approach of some boss; the shouting of the peons " throwing " a laden car along the track through the heavy smoke-laden air, so thick with the smell of powder and thin with oxygen that even experienced bosses developed raging headaches, and the Beau Brummel secretary of the company fell down once with dizziness and went to bed after the weekly inspection.

When the first day was done I carried the ten sacks of samples — via Bruno's shoulders — through the labyrinth of corridors and shafts to be loaded on a car and pushed to the main shaft, where blew a veritable sea-breeze that gave those coming from the red-hot pockets a splendid chance for catching cold which few overlooked. In the *bodega*, or underground office, I changed my dripping garments

One of Mexico's countless "armies"

Vendors of strawberries at the station of Irapuato

for dry ones, but waited long for the broken-down motor to lift me again finally to pure air. In the days that followed I was advanced to the rank of car-boss in this same level, and found enough to do and more in keeping the tricky car-men moving. A favorite ruse was to tip over a car on its way to the chute and to grunt and groan over it for a half-hour pretending to lift it back on the rails; or to tuck away far back in some abandoned " lead " the cars we needed, until I went on tours of investigation and ferreted them out.

During the last days of October I drew my car-boss wages and set out to follow the ore after it left the mine. From the underground chutes it was drawn up to the surface in the iron buckets, dumped on " gridleys " (screens made of railroad rails separated a like width) after weighing, broken up and the worthless rock thrown out on the " dump," a great artificial hill overhanging the valley below and threatening to bury the little native houses huddled down in it. A toy Baldwin locomotive dragged the ore trains around the hill to the noisy stamp-mill spreading through another valley, with a village of adobe huts overgrown with masses of purple flowers and at the bottom a plain of white sand waste from which the " values " had been extracted. The last samples I had taken assayed nine pounds of silver and 23 grams of gold to the ton. The carloads were dumped into bins at the top of the mill.

The nature of the country had been taken advantage of in the building, which hung twelve stories high on the steep hillside, making gravitation the chief means of transportation during the refining process. Rocks were screened into one receptacle and broken up by hand. The finer stuff went direct to the stamps. Stones of ordinary size were spread by machinery on a broad leather belt that passed three peon women, who picked out and tossed away the oreless stones. Their movements were leisurely, but they were sharp-eyed and very few worthless bits got by the three of them. A story below, the picked material went under deafening stamps weighing tons and striking several blows a second, while water was turned in to soften the material. This finally ran down another story in liquid form into huge cylinders where it was rolled and rolled again and at last flowed on, smelling like mortar or wet lime, onto platforms of zinc constantly shaking as with the ague and with water steadily flowing over them. Workmen about the last and most concentrated of these were locked in rooms made of chicken-wire. Below, the stuff flowed into enormous vats, like giants' washtubs, and was stirred and watered here for several days until the "values" had settled and were drawn off at the bottom. There were three stories, or some thirty, of these immense vats. The completed process left these full of white sand which a pair of peons spent several days shoveling out and carrying down into the valley.

The " values " were next run down into smaller vats and treated with zinc shavings, precipitating a 50 per cent. pure metal, black in color, which was put into melting-pots in a padlocked room overseen by an American. Here it was cast in large brick molds, these being knocked off and the metal left to slack, after which it was melted again and finally turned into gray-black blocks of the size and form of a paving-brick, 85 per cent. pure, about as heavy as the average lady would care to lift, and worth something like $1250 each. Two or four of these were tied on the back of a donkey and a train of them driven under guard to the town office, whence they were shipped to Mexico City, and finally made into those elusive things called coins, or sundry articles for the vainglorious, shipped abroad or stolen by revolutionists. On this same ground the old colonial Spaniards used to spread the ore in a cobbled patio, treat it with mercury, and drive mules round and round in it for weeks until they pocketed whatever was left to them after paying the king's fifth and the tithes of the church.

My rucksack on the back of a peon — and it is astonishing how much more easily one's possessions carry in that fashion; as if it were indeed that automatic baggage on legs I have long contemplated

inventing—I set off to the neighboring mine of
" Peregrina." As the peon was accustomed to carry
anything short of a grand piano, he did not complain
at this half-day excursion under some twenty pounds.
Being drawn out, he grew quite cheery on this new
fashion of carrying—" when the load is not much."
In the cool morning air, with a wind full of ozone
sweeping across the high country, the trail lay across
tumbled stretches of rocky ground, range behind
range of mountains beyond and a ruined stone hut
or corral here and there carrying the memory back
to Palestine. For a half hour we had Guanajuato
in full sight in its narrow gully far below. Many
donkeys pattered by under their loads of encinal
fagots, the ragged, expressionless drivers plodding
silently at their heels.

Ahead grew the roar of " Peregrina's " stamp-mill,
and I was soon winding through the gorge-hung
village. According to the manager, I had chosen
well the time of my coming, for there was " something doing." We strolled about town until he had
picked up the jefe político, a handsome Mexican,
built as massive as an Aztec stone idol, under a veritable haystack of hat, who ostensibly at least was a
sworn friend of the mining company. With him we
returned to the deafening stamp-mill and brought
up in the " zinc room," where the metal is cast into
bricks. Here the stealing of ore by workmen is
particularly prevalent, and even the searching by

the trusty at the gate not entirely effective, for even the skimming off of the scum leaves the floor scattered with chips of silver with a high percentage of gold which even the American in charge cannot always keep the men from concealing. Hence there occurs periodically the scene we were about to witness.

When the native workmen of the "zinc room" enter for the day, they are obliged to strip in one chamber and pass on to the next to put on their working clothes, reversing the process when they leave. To-day all five of them were herded together in one dressing-room, of which, the three of us being admitted, the door was locked. The jefe político, as the government authority of the region, set about searching them, and as his position depended on the good-will of the powerful mining company, it was no perfunctory "frisking." The ragged fellows were called up one by one and ordered to strip of blouses, shirts, and trousers, and even *borrachas*, their flat leather sandals, the jefe examining carefully even the seams of their garments. Indeed, he even searched the hairs of their bodies for filings of "high-grade."

The men obeyed with dog-like alacrity, though three of them showed some inner emotion, whether of guilt, fear, or shame, it was hard to guess. Two had been carefully gone over without the discovery of anything incriminating, when the jefe suddenly snatched up the hat of the first and found in it a knotted handkerchief containing a scrap of pure metal some two inches long. From then on his luck increased. The fourth man had been fidgeting about, half disrobing before the order came, when all at once the local authority turned and picked up a piece of ore as large as a silver dollar, wrapped in paper, which the fellow had surreptitiously tossed away among a bunch of mats against the wall. The jefe cuffed him soundly and ordered him to take off his shoes — he was the only one of the five sporting that luxury — and discovered in the toe of one of them a still larger booty. The last of the group was a cheery little fellow barely four feet high, likable in spite of his ingrained lifetime lack of soap. He showed no funk, and when ordered to undress turned to the " gringo " manager with: " Me too, jefe? " Then he quickly stripped, proving himself not only honest but the biggest *little* giant imaginable. He had a chest like a wine-barrel and legs that resembled steel poles, weighed fifty-two kilos, yet according to the manager, of whom he was one of the trusties, frequently carried four-hundred-pound burdens up the long hill below the mine. The jefe found something tied up in his old red cloth belt, but little Barrel-chest never lost his smile, and the suspicious lump proved to be a much-folded old chromo print of some saint.

" What 's he got that for? " asked the manager.

"To save him from the devil," sneered the jefe, wadding it up and tossing it back at him.

When he was dressed again the little giant was sent to town for policemen, a sign of confidence which seemed greatly to please him. For a half hour we smoked and joked and discussed, like so many cattle in the shambles, the three prisoners, two found guilty and the third suspected, who stood silent and motionless against the wall. Three policemen in shoddy uniforms, armed with clubs and enormous revolvers sticking out through their short coat-tails, at length appeared, of the same class and seeming little less frightened than the prisoners. They were ordered to tie ropes about the waists of the criminals and stood clutching these and the tails of the red sarapes, when the jefe interrupted some anecdote to shout the Spanish version of:

"What in —— are you waiting for?"

They dodged as if he had thrown a brick, and hurried their prisoners away to the cold, flea-ridden, stone calaboose of the town, where in all probability they lay several months before their case was even called up; while the manager and I ascended to his veranda and flower-grown residence and sat down to a several course dinner served by a squad of solemn servants. As in many another land, it pays to be a white man in Mexico.

Stealing is rarely a virtue. But it was not hard to put oneself in the place of these wretches and catch their point of view that made such thievery justifiable. As they saw it, these foreigners had made them go down into their own earth and dig out its treasures, paid them little for their labors, and searched them whenever they left that they should not keep even a little bit of it for themselves. Now they had made their own people shut them up because they had picked up a few dollars' worth of scraps left over from the great burro-loads of which, to their notion, the hated " gringoes " were robbing them. Like the workingmen of England, they were only " getting some of their own back." They were no doubt more " aficionados al pulque " and gambling than to their families, but so to some extent were the " gringoes " also, and they were by no means the only human beings who would succumb to the same temptation under the same circumstances.

The ancient " Peregrina " mine was different from " Pingüico." Here we entered by a level opening and walked down most of the two thousand feet, much of it by narrow, slimy, slippery, stone steps, in some places entirely worn away by the bare feet of the many generations of peons that as slaves to the Spaniards of colonial days used to carry the ore up on their backs from the very bottom of the mine. " Peregrina " mountain was almost another Mammoth Cave, so enormous are the caverns that have been " stoped out " of it in the past four centuries. In many a place we could see even with several can-

The wall of Guadalajara penitentiary against which prisoners are shot

The liver-shaking stage-coach from Atequisa to Chapala

dles only the ground underfoot and perhaps a bit of the nearest sidewall; the rest was a dank, noiseless, blank space, seeming square miles in extent. For three hours we wandered up and down and in and out of huge unseen caves, now and then crawling up or down three or four hundred foot " stopes " on hands and knees, by ladders, stone steps, or toe-holes in the rock. Through it all it was raining much of the time in torrents — in the mine, that is, for outside the sun was shining brightly — with mud underfoot and streams of water running along much of the way; and, unlike the sweltering interior of " Pingüico," there was a dank dungeon chill that reached the marrow of the bones. Even in the shafts which we descended in buckets, cold water poured down upon us, and, far from being naked, the miners wore all the clothing they possessed. Here the terror of the peons was an old American mine-boss rated " loco " among them, who went constantly armed with an immense and ancient re-volver, always loaded and reputed of " hair trigger," which he drew and whistled in the barrel whenever he wished to call a workman. A blaze crackling in the fireplace was pleasant during the evening in the man-ager's house, for " Peregrina " lies even higher above the sea than " Pingüico "; but even here by night or day the peons, and especially the women, went bare-foot and in thinnest garb.

A native horse, none of which seem noted for their

speed, carried me out to the famous old mining town
of La Luz, where the Spaniards first began digging
in this region. The animal made little headway
forward, but fully replaced this by the distance covered up and down. To it a trot was evidently an
endeavor to see how many times and how high it
could jump into the air from the same spot. The
ancient Aztecs, seeing us advancing upon them,
would never have made the mistake of fancying man
and horse parts of the same animal. Moreover, the
pesky beast had an incurable predilection for tread-
ing, like a small boy "showing off," the extreme edge
of pathways at times not six inches from a sheer fall
of from five hundred to a thousand feet down rock-
faced precipices.

Still it was a pleasant three-hour ride in the brilliant sunshine, winding round and over the hills along
pitching and tossing trails. Peons obsequiously
lifted their hats when I passed, which they do not to
a man afoot; a solemn stillness of rough-and-tumble
mountains and valleys, with deep-shadowed little
gorges scolloped out of the otherwise sun-flooded
landscape, broad hedges of cactus and pitching
paths, down which the animal picked its way with
ease and assurance, alternated with mighty climbs
over a dozen rises, each of which I fancied the last.

La Luz is a typical town of mountainous Mexico.
A long, broken adobe village lies scattered along a
precipitous valley, scores of "roads" and trails

hedged with cactus wind and swoop and climb again
away over steep hills and through deep *barrancos*,
troops of peons and donkeys enlivening them; flowers
give a joyful touch, and patches of green and the
climate help to make the place reminiscent of the
more thickly settled portions of Palestine. From
the town we could see plainly the city of Leon,
fourth in Mexico, and a view of the plain, less striking than that from " Pingüico," because of the range
rising to cut it off in the middle distance. The
mountains of all this region are dotted with round,
white, cement monuments, the boundary marks of
different mining properties. By Mexican law each
must be visible from the adjoining two, and in this
pitched and tumbled country this requires many.

Beyond the village we found, about the old Spanish workings, ancient, roofless, stone buildings with
loop-holed turrets for bandits and nitches for saints.
These structures, as well as the waste dumped by
the Spaniards, were being " repicked for values,"
and broken up and sent through the stamp-mill, the
never-ending rumble of which sounded incessantly,
like some distant water-fall; for with modern methods
it pays to crush rock with even a few dollars a ton
value in it, and the Americans of to-day mine much
that the Spaniards with their crude methods cast
aside or did not attempt to work. At a mine in the
vicinity the ancient, stone mansion serving as residence of the superintendent was torn down and sent

through the stamping-mill, and a new one of less valuable rock erected.   We descended 1600 feet into the mine of La Luz down a perfectly round, stone-lined shaft in a small iron bucket held by a one-inch wire cable and entirely in charge of peons — who fortunately either had nothing against us or did not dare to vent it.

CHAPTER IV

ROUND ABOUT LAKE CHAPALA

WITH the coming of November I left Guanajuato behind. The branch line down to
Silao was soon among broad plains of corn, without rocks even along the flat, ragged, country roads,
bringing to mind that it was long since I had walked
on level and unobstructed ground. The crowding
of the second-class car forced me to share a
bench with a chorus girl of the company that had
been castilianizing venerable Broadway favorites in
Guanajuato's chief theater. She was about forty,
looked it with compound interest, was graced with
the form of a Panteón mummy, and a face — but
some things are too horrible even to be mentioned in
print. Most of the way she wept copiously, apparently at some secret a pocket mirror insisted on re-
peating to her as often as she drew it out, and re-
gained her spirits only momentarily during the
smoking of each of several cigarettes. Finally she
took to saying her beads in a sepulchral, moaning
voice, her eyes closed, and wagging her head from
side to side in the rhythm of her professional calling,

until we pulled into the one-story, adobe, checker-board town.   All the troupe except the two " stars " rode second-class, dressed much like peons, and carried their possessions in misshapen bundles under their arms.   If the one performance I had seen was typical, this was far better treatment than they deserved.

The express from El Paso and the North set me down in the early night at Irapuato, out of the darkness of which bobbed up a dozen old women, men, and boys with wailing cries of " Fresas! "   For this is the town of perennial strawberries.   The basket of that fruit heaped high and fully a foot in diameter which sat before me next morning as we rambled away westward toward Guadalajara cost *cuatro reales* — a quarter, and if the berries grew symmetrically smaller toward the bottom, an all-day appetite by no means brought to light the tiniest. The way lay across a level land bathed in sunshine, of extreme fertility, and watered by harnessed streams flowing down from the distant hills.   All the day one had a sense of the richness of nature, not the prodigality of the tropics to make man indolent, but just sufficient to give full reward for reasonable exertion.   The rich, black, fenceless plains were burnished here and there with little shallow lakes of the rainy season, and musical with wild birds of many species.   Primitive well-sweeps punctuated the landscape, and now and then the church towers of some adobe village peered through the mesquite trees. In the afternoon grazing grew more frequent and herds of cattle and flocks of goats populated all the scene. Within the car and without, the hats of the peons, with all their sameness, were never exactly alike. Each bore some individuality, be it in shape, shade, material, or manner of wearing, as distinct as among the fair sex in other lands; and that without resorting to decorating them with flowers, vegetables, or dead birds. Some wore around them ribbons with huge letters proposing, " Viva ——" this or that latest aspirant to the favor of the primitive-minded " pela'o," but these were always arranged in a manner to add to rather than detract from the artistic ensemble. Many a young woman of the same class was quite attractive in appearance, though thick bulky noses robbed all of the right to be called beautiful. They did not lose their charms, such as they were, prematurely, as do so many races of the South, and the simplicity of dress and hair arrangement added much to the pleasing general effect.

As night descended we began to pant upward through low hills, wooded, but free from the rocks and boulders of a mining region, and in the first darkness drew up at Guadalajara, second city of Mexico. It is a place that adorns the earth. Jalisco State, of which this is the capital, has been called the Andalusia of Mexico, and the city is in-

deed a Seville of the West, though lacking in her
spontaneity of life, for this cruder people is much
more tempered with a constant fear of betraying
their crudeness and in consequence much weighed
down by " propriety." But its bright, central plaza
has no equal to the north. Here as the band plays
amid the orange trees heavy with ripening fruit, the
more haughty of the population promenade the inner square, outside which stroll the peons and " lower
classes "; though only custom seems responsible for
the division. One misses in Mexico the genuine democracy of Spain. The idea of a conquered race still
holds, and whoever has a strain of white in his veins
— or even in the hue of his collar — considers it
fitting to treat the Indian mass with a cold, indifferent tone of superiority. Yet in the outer circle the
unprejudiced observer found more pleasing than
within. One was reminded of Mark Twain's suggestion that complexions of some color wear best in
tropical lands. In this, above all, the women of the
rebozo were vastly superior to those who stepped
from their carriages at about the beginning of the
third number and took to parading, the two sexes in
pairs marching in opposite directions at a snail's
pace. The "women of the people" had more sense
of the fitness of things than to ape the wealthy in
dress, like the corresponding class in our own land,
and their simplicity of attire stood out in attractive

Lake Chapala from the estate of Ribero Castellanos

The head farmer of the estate under an aged fig-tree

contrast to the pasty features and unexercised figures in " Parisian " garb of the inner circle.

Guadalajara has the requisites of a real city. Its streets are well paved with macadam, and it even possesses garbage wagons. Indeed, in some respects it has carried " progress " too far, as in the case of the winking electric sign of Broadway proportions advertising a *camisería* — a local " shirtery," before which fascinated peons from the distant villages stand gazing as at one of the seven wonders of the universe. Beggars are few and there is none of the oppressive poverty of other Mexican cities. This, it is agreed, is due not merely to the extreme fertility of Jalisco, but to the kindness of nature in refusing to produce the maguey in the vicinity, so that drunkenness is at its lowest Mexican ebb and the sour stink of pulque shops nowhere assails the nostrils. For this curse of the peon will not endure long transportation. An abundance of cheap labor makes possible many little conveniences unknown in more industrial lands, and the city has a peaceful, soothing air and temperature, due perhaps to its ideal altitude of six thousand feet, that makes life drift along like a pleasant dream.

But its nights are hideous. The Mexican seems to relish constant uproar, and if Guadalajara is ever to be the open-air health resort for frayed nerves and weakened lungs it aspires to, there must come a diligent suppression of unnecessary noises. As the evening gathering evaporates, leaving the plaza sprinkled with a few dreamy mortals and scattered policemen eating the lunch their wives bring and share with them, pandemonium seems to be released from its confinement. First these same preservers of law and order take to blowing their hair-raising whistles at least every ten minutes from one to another back and forth through every street, as if mutually to keep up their courage. Scores of the gilded youth on the way home from " playing the bear " before their favorite *rejas* join together in bands to howl their glee at the kindness of life into the small hours, the entire stock of street-cars seems to be sent out nightly on some extended excursion with orders never to let their gongs fall silent, and long before dawn even the few who have succeeded in falling into a doze are snatched awake by an atrocious din of church-bells sufficient in number to supply heaven, nirvana, the realm of houris, and the Irish section of purgatory, with enough left over to furnish boiling pots for the more crowded section of the Hereafter. Then with a dim suggestion of dawn every living dog and fighting-cock, of which each inhabitant appears to possess at least a score, joins the forty-thousand vendors of forty thousand different species of uselessness howling in at least as many different voices and tones, each a bit louder than all the others, until even an unoccupied wanderer concludes that sleep is an idle waste of an all too short existence.

I brought up a day of random wandering in state's prison. The *Penitenciaria* of Guadalajara is a huge, wheel-shaped building in the most modern style of that class of architecture. The bullet-headed youth in soldier's uniform and the complexion of a long-undusted carpet, leaning on his musket at the entrance, made no move to halt me, and I stepped forth on a patio forested with orange trees, to find that most of the public had preceded me, including some hundred fruit, tortilla, cigarette, and candy vendors. Here was no sign of prisoners. I approached another stern boy armed like a first-class cruiser in war time and he motioned upward with his gun barrel. The dwelling of the *comandante* faced the patio on the second-story corridor. His son, aged five, met me with the information:

" Papá 'stá dormido."

But he was misinformed, for when his mother introduced me into the parlor, father, in shirt-sleeves, was already rubbing the sleep out of his eyes and preparing to light the first after-siesta cigarette. When my impressiveness had penetrated his re-awakening intellect, he prepared me a document which, reduced to succinct English, amounted to the statement that the prison and all it contained was mine for the asking.

A whiff of this sesame opened like magic the three

immense iron doors through anterooms in charge
of trusties, in prison garb of the material of blue
overalls and caps shaped like a low fez. Inside, a
" preso de confianza " serving as turnkey led the way
along a great stone corridor to a little central patio
with flowers and a central fountain babbling mer-
rily. From this radiated fifteen other long-vaulted
passages, seeming each fully a half mile in length;
for with Latin love of the theatrical the farther ends
had been painted to resemble an endless array of
cells, even the numbers being continued above the
false doors to minute infinity. Besides these imaginary ones there were some forty real places of confinement on each side of each coridor, three-cornered,
stone rooms with a comfortable cot and noticeable
cleanliness. The hundred or more convicts, wandering about or sitting in the sun of the patio, were
only locked in them by night. Whenever we entered
a corridor or a room, two strokes were sounded on
a bell and all arose and stood at attention until we
had passed. Yet the discipline was not oppressive,
petty matters being disregarded. The corridor of
those condemned to be shot was closed with an iron-
barred gate, but the inmates obeyed with alacrity
when my guide ordered them to step forth to be photographed.

One of the passageways led to the *talleres* or
workshops, also long and vaulted and well-lighted by
windows high up in the curve of the arched roof.

These showed the stone walls to be at least four
feet thick, yet the floor was of earth.   On it along
the walls sat men weaving straw ribbons to be sewn
into hats on the American sewing-machines beyond.
In side rooms were blacksmith, carpenter, and tin-
smith shops in which all work was done by hand,
the absence of machinery suggesting to the trusty in
charge that Mexico is " muy pobre " as compared
with other lands.   Convicts were obliged to work
seven hours a day.   Scattered through the building
were several small patios with patches of sun, in
which many prisoners were engaged in making in-
genious little knickknacks which they were permitted
to sell for their own benefit.   The speciality of one
old fellow under life sentence was a coin purse with
the slightly incongruous device, " Viva la Inde-
pendencia ! "

There was a complete absence of vicious faces, at
least faces more so than those of the great mass of
peons outside.   I recalled the assertions of cynical American residents that all Mexicans are criminals and that those in jail were only the ones who
have had the misfortune to get caught.   Certainly
there was nothing in their outward appearance to
distinguish the inmates from any gathering of the
same class beyond prison walls.   Off one corridor
opened the bath patio, large, and gay with sunshine
and flowers, with a large swimming pool and several
smaller baths.   The prisoners are required to bathe

at least every Sunday. Within the penitentiary was
a garden of several acres, on the walls above which
guards patroled with loaded muskets and in which
prisoners raised every species of fruit and vegetable
known in the region. The institution indeed was
fully self-supporting. The kitchen was lined with
huge vats into which bushels of beans, corn, and the
like were shoveled, and like the prison tailor, shoe,
and barber shops, was kept in excellent order. Several short-time prisoners, among them many boys,
volunteered to stand in appropriate attitudes before
the heavy wall at the end of a three-cornered court
where condemned men are shot at three paces in the
dawn of many an early summer day. In one corridor the prison band, entirely made up of prisoners,
was practising, and when I had been seated in state
on a wooden bench they struck up several American
favorites, ending with our national hymn, all played
with the musical skill common to the Mexican Indian,
even among those unable to read a note. On the
whole the prison was as cheery and pleasant as fitted
such an institution, except the women's ward, into
which a vicious-looking girl admitted me sulkily at
sight of the comandante's order. A silent, nonde-
script woman of forty took me in charge with all too
evident ill-will and marched me around the patio on
which opened the rooms of female inmates, while
the fifty or more of them left off their cooking and
washing for the male prisoners and stood at dis-

gruntled attention in sullen silence. Their quarters
were noticeably dirtier than those of the men. My
guide took leave of me at the first of the three iron
doors, having still to postpone his exit a year or
more, and these again, fortunately, swung on their
hinges as if by magic to let pass only one of the thousand of us within.

On the mule-car that dragged and jolted us out
to the "Niagara of Mexico" were three resident
Germans who strove to be "simpático" to the natives by a clumsy species of "horse play." Their
asininity is worth mention only because among those
laughing at their antics was a peon who had been
gashed across the hand, half-severing his wrist, yet
who sat on the back platform without even a rag
around the wound, though with a rope tourniquet
above. Two gray and decrepit policemen rode with
him and half way out stopped at a stone hut to arrest the perpetrator of the deed and bring him along,
wrapped in the customary red sarape and indifference.

The waterfall over a broad face of rock was pleasing but not extraordinary, and swinging on my rucksack I struck off afoot. The lightly rolling land was
very fertile, with much corn, great droves of cattle,
and many shallow lakes, its climate a pleasant cross
between late spring and early fall. From El
Castillo the path lay along the shimmering railroad,
on which I outdid the train to Atequisa station.

The orange vendors lolling here under the shade of
their hats gave the distance to Chapala as fifteen
miles, and advised me to hire a horse or take passage
in the stage. This primitive bone-shaker, dark-red
in color, the body sitting on huge leather springs,
was drawn by four teams of mules in tandem, and before revolution spread over the land was customarily
packed to the roof and high above it with excursion-
ists to Mexico's chief inland watering-place. Now
it dashed back and forth almost empty.

I preferred my own legs. A soft road led between orange-groves — at the station were offered
for sale seedless oranges compared to which those of
California are pigmies — to the drowsing town of
Atequisa. Through one of its crumbling stone gates
the way spread at large over its sandy, sun-bathed
plaza, then contracted again to a winding wide trail,
rising leisurely into the foothills beyond. A farmer
of sixty, homeward bound to his village of Santa
Cruz on a loose-eared ass, fell in with me. He lacked
entirely that incommunicative manner and half-re-
sentful air I had so often encountered in the Mexican, and his country dialect whiled away the time as
we followed the unfenced " road " around and slowly
upward into hills less rugged than those about
Guanajuato and thinly covered with coarse grass
and small brush. Twenty-one years ago he had
worked here as *mozo* for " gringoes," my compatriots.
They had offered him a whole peso a day if he would

A Mexican village

not get married.   But "he and she both wanted,"
so "qué quiera usté' "?   They had started farming
on a little piece of rocky ridge.   He would point it
out to me when we came nearer.   By and by he had
bought another piece of land for fifty pesos and then
poco á poco for forty pesos some more.   Then for
twenty-four pesos and fifty centavos he had bought a
cow, and the *vaca* before long gave them a fine calf
and twelve *cuartillos* of milk a day.   So that he was
able to buy another heifer and then an ox and finally
another ox and —

Whack!   It took many a thump and prod and
"Bur-r-r-r-r-r-o!" to make the pretty little mouse-
colored donkey he was riding keep up with me — and
what did I think he paid for him?   Eighteen pesos!
Sí, señor, ní más ní menos.   A bargain, eh?   And
for the other one at home, which is larger, only
twenty-two pesos, and for the one *they* stole from
him, fifteen pesos and a bag of corn.   And once *they*
stole all three of the *burritos* and he ran half way to
Colima and had them arrested and got the *animalitos*
back.   So that now he had two oxen — pray God
they were still safe — and two burros and three
pieces of land and a good wife — only yesterday she
fell down and broke her arm and he had had to cut
sticks to tie it up and she would have to work without using it for a long time —

Whack!   "Anda bur-r-r-r-r-ro!" and once he
owned it he never could get himself to sell an ani-

malito. They were sometimes useful to plow and
plant anyway, and this life of *sembrar* and *cosechar*
was just the one for him. The cities, bah! — though
he had been twice to Guadalajara and only too glad
to get away again — and was n't I tired enough to
try the burrito a while, I should find her pace smooth
as sitting on the ground. No? Well, at least if I
got tired I could come and spend the night in his
casita, a very poor little house, to be sure, which he
had built himself long ago, soon after they were married, but there I would be in my own house, and his
wife — or perhaps now he himself — would *ordeñar*
la vaca and there would be fresh milk and —

So on for some seven or eight miles. Here and
there the road passed through an open gate as into
a farmyard, though there were no adjoining fences
to mark these boundaries of some new hacienda or
estate. From the highest point there was a pretty
retrospect back on Atequisa and the railroad and the
broad valley almost to far-off Guadalajara, and
ahead, also still far away, Lake Chapala shimmering
in the early sunset. Between lay broad, rolling land,
rich with flowers and shrubbery, and with much cultivation also, one vast field of ripening Indian corn
surely four miles long and half as wide stretching
like a sea to its surrounding hills, about its edge the
leaf and branch shacks of its guardians. Maize, too,
covered all the slope down to the mountain-girdled
lake, and far, far away on a point of land, like Tyre

out in the Mediterranean, the twin towers of the
church of Chapala stood out against the dimming
lake and the blue-gray range beyond.

Two leagues off it the peasant pointed out the
ridge that hid his casita and his animalitos and his
good wife — with her broken arm now — and regret-
ting that I would not accept his poor hospitality,
for I must be tired, he rode away down a little bar-
ranca walled by tall bushes with brilliant masses of
purple, red, and pink flowers and so on up to the
little patch of corn which — yes, surely, I could see
a corner of it from here, and from it, if only I would
come, I should see the broad blue view of Chapala
lake, and — My road descended and went down
into the night, plentifully scattered with loose stones.
Before it had grown really dark I found myself casting a shadow ahead, and turned to find an enormous
red moon gazing dreamily at me from the summit of
the road behind.   Then came the suburbs and enormous ox-carts loaded with everything, and donkeys
without number passing silent-footed in the sand, and
peons, lacking entirely the half-insolence and pulque-
sodden faces of Guanajuato region, greeted me un-
failingly with " Adiós " or " Buenas noches."

But once in the cobble-paved village I must pay
high in the " Hotel Victor "— the larger ones being
closed since anarchy had confined the wealthy to their
cities — for a billowy bed and a chicken centuries
old served by waiters in evening dress and trained-

monkey manners.   The free and easy old *casa de
asistencia* of Guadalajara was far more to my liking.
But at least the landlord loaned me a pair of trunks
for a moonlight swim in Lake Chapala, whispering
some secret to its sandy beaches in the silence of the
silver-flooded night.

It is the largest lake in Mexico, second indeed only
to Titicaca among the lofty sheets of water of the
Western world.   More than five thousand feet above
the sea, it is shallow and stormy as Lake Erie.
Waves were dashing high at the foot of the town
in the morning.   Its fishermen are ever fearful of
its fury and go to pray for a safe return from every
trip before their patron St. Peter in the twin-spired
village church up toward which the lake was surging
this morning as if in anger that this place of refuge
should be granted its legitimate victims.

Its rage made the journey by water I had planned
to Ribera Castellanos inadvisable, even had an owner
of one of the little open boats of the fishermen been
willing to trust himself on its treacherous bosom, and
by blazing eleven I was plodding back over the road
of yesterday.   The orange vendors of Atequisa
gathered around me at the station, marveling at the
strength of my legs.   In the train I shared a bench
with a dignified old Mexican of the country regions,
who at length lost his reserve sufficiently to tell me
of the " muy amigo gringo " whose picture he still
had on the wall of his house since the day twenty-

seven years ago when my compatriot had stopped with him on a tour of his native State, carrying a small pack of merchandise which gave him the entrée into all houses, but which he purposely held at so high a price that none would buy.

From Ocotlán station a broad level highway, from which a glimpse is had of the sharp, double peak of Colima volcano, runs out to Ribera Castellanos. Sam Rogers was building a tourist hotel there. Its broad lawn sloped down to the edge of Lake Chapala, lapping at the shores like some smaller ocean; from its verandas spread a view of sixty miles across the Mexican Titicaca, with all vacation sports, a perennial summer without undue heat, and such sunsets as none can describe. The hacienda San Andrés, also American owned, embraced thousands of acres of rich bottom land on which already many varieties of fruit were producing marvelously, as well as several mountain peaks and a long stretch of lake front. The estate headquarters was like some modern railway office, with its staff of employees. In the nearby stables horses were saddled for us and we set off for a day's trip all within the confines of the farm, under guidance of the bulky Mexican head overseer in all his wealth of national garb and armament.

For miles away in several directions immense fields were being plowed by dozens of ox-teams, the white garments of the drivers standing out sharply against the brown landscape. Two hours' riding around the lagoon furnishing water for irrigation brought us to a village of some size, belonging to the estate. The wife of one of the bee-tenders emerged from her hut with bowls of clear rich honey and tortillas, and the manner of a serf of medieval times before her feudal lord. The bees lived in hollow logs with little thatched roofs. For several miles more the rich bottom lands continued. Then we began to ascend through bushy foothills, and cultivation dropped behind us, as did the massive head overseer, whose weight threatened to break his horse's back. Well up we came upon the " chaparral," the hacienda herdsman, tawny with sunburn even to his leather garments. He knew by name every animal under his charge, though the owners did not even know the number they possessed. A still steeper climb, during the last of which even the horses had to be abandoned, brought us to a hilltop overlooking the entire lake, with the villages on its edge, and range after range of the mountains of Jalisco and Michoacán. Our animals were more than an hour picking their way down the stony trails between all but perpendicular cornfields, the leaves of which had been stripped off to permit the huge ear at the top the more fully to ripen. A boulder set in motion at the top of a field would have been sure death to the man or horse it struck at the bottom.

The hotel launch set me across the lake next morn-

ing. From the rock-tumbled fisher-town of La
Palma an arriero pointed out to me far away across
the plains of Michoacán a mountain of striking re-
semblance to Mt. Tabor in Palestine, as the land-
mark on the slopes of which to seek that night's
lodging. The treeless land of rich black loam was
flat as a table, yet the trail took many a turn, now to
avoid the dyke of a former governor and Porfirio
Diaz, who planned to pump dry this end of the lake,
now for some reason only those with Mexican blood
in their veins could fathom. Peons were fishing in
the irrigating ditches with machetes, laying their
huge, sluggish victims all but cut in two on the grass
behind them.

Noon brought Sahuayo, a large village in an
agricultural district, in one of the huts of which ten
cents produced soup, pork, frijoles, tortillas, and
coffee, to say nothing of the tablecloth in honor of so
unexpected a guest and a dozen oranges for the
thirst beyond. The new trail struck off across the
fields almost at right angles to the one that had
brought me. I was already on the hacienda Guara-
cha, largest of the State of Michoacán, including
within its holdings a dozen such villages as this, but
the owner to whom I bore a letter lived still leagues
distant. Dwellers on the estate must labor on it
when required or seek residence elsewhere, which
means far distant. All with whom I spoke on the

subject, native or foreigners, seemed agreed that the peon prefers this plan to being thrown on his own responsibility.

The traveler could easily fancy himself in danger in this vast fenceless and defenseless space. Enormous herds were visible for miles in every direction, bulls roamed here and there, bellowing moodily, cattle and horses by hundreds waded and grazed in the shallow swamps across which the dyked path led. All the brilliant day " Mt. Tabor " stood forth in all its beauty across the plain in this clear air, and the sun brought sweat even at more than a mile above the sea.

I was in the very heart of Birdland. These broad, table-flat stretches of rich plateau, now half inundated, seemed some enormous outdoor aviary. Every species of winged creature one had hoped ever to see even in Zoo cages or the cases of museums seemed here to live and fly and have its songful being. Great sluggish *sopilotes* of the horrid vulture family strolled or circled lazily about, seeking the scent of carrion. Long-legged, snow-white herons stood in the marshes. Great flocks of small black birds that could not possibly have numbered less than a hundred thousand each rose and fell and undulated in waves and curtains against the background of mountains beyond, screening it as by some great black veil. There were blood-red birds, birds blue as turquoise, some of almost lilac hue, every grassy pond was over-

Making glazed floor tiles on a Mexican estate

Vast seas of Indian corn stretch to pine-clad hills, while around
them are guard-shacks at frequent intervals

spread with wild ducks so tame they seemed waiting
to be picked up and caressed, eagles showed off their
spiral curves in the sky above like daring aviators
over some admiring field of spectators; everywhere
the stilly hum of semi-tropical life was broken only
by the countless and inimitable bird calls.

As my shadow grew ungainly, the dyked path
struck across a long wet field against the black soil
of which the dozens of white-clad peons with their
mattocks gleamed like grains of rice on an ebony surface.   Beyond, it entered foothills, flanked a peak,
and joined a wide road leading directly to an immense cluster of buildings among trees.   The sun
was firing the western horizon.   From every direction groups of white-garbed peons were drawing like
homing pigeons toward this center of the visible
landscape.   I reached it with them and, passing
through several massive gates, mounted through a
corral or cobbled stable yard with many bulky, two-
wheeled carts and fully two hundred mules, then up
an inclined, cobbled way through a garden of flowers
to the immense pillared veranda with cement floor of
the owner's hacienda residence.

The building was in the form of a hollow square,
enclosing a flowery patio as large as many a town
plaza.   Don Diego was not at home, nor indeed were
any of his immediate family, who preferred the ur-
ban pleasures of Guadalajara.   The Indian door-
tender brought me to " Don Carlos," a fat, cheerful

man of forty in a white jacket, close-fitting trousers, and an immense revolver attached to the left side of his broad and heavily weighted cartridge-belt. I presented my letter of introduction from an American friend of the owner and was soon entangled in the coils of Mexican pseudo-politeness. Don Carlos tore himself away from his priceless labors as manager of the hacienda and took me up on the flat roof of the two-story house, from which a fine view was had for miles in all directions; indeed, nearly a half of the estate could be seen, with its peon villages, its broad stretches of new-plowed fields, and the now smokeless chimney of the sugar mill among the trees.

The interest of the manager did not extend beyond the cut-and-dried formalities common to all Mexicans. In spite of his honeyed words, it was evident he looked upon me as a necessary evil, purposely come to the hacienda to seek food and lodging, and to be gotten rid of as soon as possible, compatible with the sacred Arabian rules of hospitality. I had not yet learned that a letter of introduction in Latin America, given on the slightest provocation, is of just the grade of importance such custom would warrant. Not that Don Carlos was rude. Indeed, he strove outwardly to be highly *simpático*. But one read the insincerity underneath by a kind of intuition, and longed for the abrupt but honestly frank Texan.

The two front corners of the estate residence were

taken up by the hacienda store and church respectively — a handy arrangement by virtue of which
whatever went out the pay window to the peons (and
it was not much) came in again at one or the other
of the corner doors. Adjoining the building and
half surrounding it was an entire village, with a flowery plaza and promenades for its inhabitants. The
owners of the estate were less churlishly selfish than
their prototypes in our own country, in that they
permitted the public, which is to say their own workmen and families, to go freely anywhere in the family
residence and its patio, except into the dwelling-
rooms proper.

When darkness came on we sat in the piazza garden overlooking the mule-yard. The evening church
service over, the estate priest came to join us, putting on his huge black " Texas " hat and lighting a
cigarette on the chapel threshold. He wore an in-
numerable series of long black robes, which still did
not conceal the fact that the curve from chest to
waist was the opposite of that common to sculptured
figures, and his hand-shake was particularly soft and
snaky. He quickly took charge of the conversation
and led it into anecdotes very few of which could be
set down by the writers of modern days, denied the
catholic privileges of old Boccaccio and Rabelais.

Toward eight supper was announced. But instead of the conversational feast amid a company of
educated Mexican men and women I had pictured to

myself during the day's tramp, I was led into a bare stone room with a long, white-clothed table, on a corner of which sat in solitary state two plates and a salt cellar. A peon waiter brought an ample, though by no means epicurean, supper, through all which Don Carlos sat smoking over his empty plate opposite me, alleging that he never ate after noonday for dread of taking on still greater weight, and striving to keep a well-bred false politeness in the voice in which he answered my few questions. He had spent a year in a college of New Jersey, but had not even learned to pronounce the name of that State. Having pointed out to me the room I was to occupy, he excused himself for a " momentito," and I have never seen him since.

Evidently horrified at the sight of a white man, even if only a " gringo," traveling on foot, the manager had insisted on lending me a horse and mozo to the railroad station of Moreno, fifteen miles distant, but still within the confines of the hacienda. It may be also that he gave orders to have me out of his sight before he rose. At any rate it was barely three when a knock at the door aroused me and by four I stumbled out into the black starlit night to find saddled for me in the mule-corral what might by a considerable stretch of the word be called a horse. The mozo was well mounted, however, and the family chauffeur, carrying in one hand a basket of eggs he had been sent to fetch the estate owner in Guadalajara, rode a magnificent white animal. Without even the formal leave-taking cup of coffee, we set off on the road to the eastward. For road in Mexico always read — at best a winding stretch of dried mud with narrow paths meandering though the smoother parts of it, the whole tumbled everywhere with stones and rocks and broken by frequent unexpected deep cracks and stony gorges. My " horse " was as striking a caricature of that species of quadruped as could have been found in an all-night search in the region, which indeed there was reason to believe had been produced in just that manner. But at least it had the advantage of being unable to keep up with my companions, leaving me alone behind in far more pleasant company.

We wound through several long peon villages, mere grass huts on the bare earth floors of which the inhabitants lay rolled up in their blankets. I had not been supplied with spurs, essential to all horsemanship in Mexico, and was compelled at thirty second intervals to prick up the jade between my legs with the point of a lead pencil, the only weapon at hand, or be left behind entirely. As the stars dimmed and the horizon ahead took on a thin gray streak, peons wrapped in their sarapes passed now and then noiselessly in their soft leather huaraches close beside me. In huts along the way frowsy, unwashed women might be heard already crushing in their stone mortars, under stone rolling-pins, maize for the morning atole and tortillas, while thick smoke began to wander lazily out from the low doorways. Swiftly it grew lighter until suddenly an immense red sun leaped full-grown above the ragged horizon ahead, just as we sighted an isolated station building in the wilderness that now surrounded us on all sides.

A two-car train rambled through a light-wooded, half-mountainous country, stopping at every collection of huts to pick up or set down a peon or two, and drew up at length in Zamora. It was a populous, flat-roofed, ill-smelling, typical Mexican city of checkerboard pattern, on the plaza of which faced the " Hotel Morelos," formerly the " Porfirio Diaz," but with that seditious name now carefully painted over. Being barely a mile above sea-level, the town has a suggestion of the tropics and the temperature of midday is distinctly noticeable.

Zamora ranks as the most fanatical spot in Michoacán, which is itself so throttled by the church that it is known as the " estado torpe," the torpid State. Its bishop is rated second in all Mexico only to that of the sacred city of Guadalupe. Here are monasteries, and monks, and nuns in seclusion, priests roam the streets in robes and vestments, form processions, and display publicly the " host " and other paraphernalia of their faith; all of which is forbidden by the laws of Mexico. When I emerged from the hotel, every person in sight, from newsboys to lawyers in frock coats, was kneeling wherever he hap-

pened to be, on his veranda, on the sidewalk, or in
the middle of the street, his hat laid on the ground
before him, facing a high churchman in flowing robes
and a " stove-pipe " hat strutting across the plaza
toward the cathedral.   Traveling priests wear their
regalia of office as far as Yurécuaro on the main line,
changing there to civilian garb.

Nor is the power of the church here confined to
things spiritual.   Vast portions of the richest sections of the State are church owned, though ostensibly property of the lawyers that control them.
Holding the reins, the ecclesiastics make it impossible
for companies to open up enterprises except under
their tutelage.   The population of the State is some
eighty per cent. illiterate, yet even foreigners find
it impossible to set up schools for their own employees.   The women *of all classes* are almost without exception illiterate.   The church refuses to edu-
cate them, and sternly forbids any one else to do so.
An American Catholic long resident reported even
the priests ignorant beyond belief, and asserted that
usury and immorality was almost universal among
the churchmen of all grades.   The peasants are
forced to give a tenth of all they produce, be it only
a patch of corn, to the church, which holds its stores
until prices are high, while the poverty-stricken peon
must sell for what he can get.   Those married by the
church are forbidden to contract the civil ceremony,
though the former is unlawful and lack of the latter

makes their children legally illegitimate. The local form of worship includes many of the barbaric superstitions of the Indians grafted on the stems of Catholicism, and weird pagan dances before the altar are a part of many a *fiesta*. The town has already churches sufficient to house easily all the population, yet an immense new cathedral is building. The purpose of its erection, according to the bishop, is " for the greater glorification of God."

I spent two days with the American superintendent of " Platanal," the electric plant run by water power a few miles out of town through fields of head-high maize. The night before my arrival bandits had raided the establishment and one of them had been killed. The president of Zamora had profusely thanked the " gringo " in charge when he presented himself in town with the body. On pay-day the manager went and came from the bank with two immense revolvers and a loaded rifle.

The current supplied by the rapids of " Platanal " is carried on high-tension wires to several cities far distant, including Guanajuato, a hundred miles away. Let the dynamo here break down and the cage of " Pingüico " mine hangs suspended in its shaft and Stygian darkness falls in the labyrinth below.   In the rainy season lightning causes much trouble, and immense flocks of birds migrating south or north, according to the period of year, keep the repair gangs busy by flying against the wires and causing short

Interior of a Mexican hut at cooking time

circuits through their dead bodies. Woodpeckers eat away the wooden cross-pieces on the iron towers with disheartening rapidity. The company is philanthropically inclined toward its employees. Even the peons are given two weeks' vacation on full pay, during which many rent a patch of land on the mountainside to plant with corn. A savings bank system is maintained, strict sanitation is insisted upon in the houses furnished by the company, and the methods of the haciendas of the region, of paying the peon the lowest possible wages for his labor and produce and selling to him at the highest possible prices at the estate store, thereby keeping him in constant debt and a species of slavery, are avoided. The result is a permanent force of high Mexican grade. All attempts of the company to introduce schools, however, even on its own property, have been frustrated by the powerful churchmen. A bright young native in the plant was an expert at figures, which he had been surreptitiously taught by his " gringo " superior, but he could not sign his name.

CHAPTER IV

MY compatriot strongly opposed my plan of walking to Uruapan — at least without an armed guard! The mountains were full of bandits, the Tarascan Indians, living much as they did at the time of the Conquest, did not even speak Spanish, they were unfriendly to whites, and above all dangerously superstitious on the subject of photography. There are persons who would consider it perilous to walk the length of Broadway, and lose sight even of the added attraction of that reputed drawback.

I was off at dawn. Hundreds of Indians from the interior had slept in scattered groups all along the road to town, beside the produce they had come to sell on market day. For it is against the law to be found out of doors in Zamora after ten! My compatriot had twice fallen foul of the vigilant police there and been roundly mulcted — once the bolt of the hired carriage in which he was riding broke, the conveyance turned turtle, mashed his foot, and covered his face with blood, and he was imprisoned and fined for "escándalo." On another occasion he spent some time in jail because his mozo behind him accidentally knocked over the lantern of a policeman set in the middle of the street.

But let us leave so straight-laced a spot behind. The rocky "road" could not hold to the same opinion for a hundred consecutive yards, but kept changing its mind as often as it caught sight of some new corner of the landscape. The Indians, who crowded the way during the first hour, were not friendly, but neither did they show any dangerous propensities, and never failed in greeting if spoken to first. There were many of them of pure aboriginal blood. The stony road climbed somewhat to gain Tangantzícuaro, then stumbled across a flatter country growing more wooded to Chilota, a large town with a tiny plaza and curious, overhanging eaves, reminiscent of Japan, stretching down its checker-board streets in all directions.

The trail, which had gone a mile or more out of its way to visit the place, no sooner left it than it fell abruptly into the bed of what in other weather would have been a rocky mountain torrent, and set off with it in a totally new direction, as if, having fallen in with congenial company, it had entirely forgotten the errand on which it had first set forth. The land was fertile, with much corn. In time road and river bed parted company, though only after several attempts, like old gossips, and the former took to climbing upward through thin forests of pine in which the wind whispered an imitation of some distant, small waterfall. For some miles there were no houses. Up and down and in and out of valleys thin with pine we wandered, with now and then a rough shelter of rubbish and thatch, halting places of traveling Indians or the guard-houses of their fields, while the sky ahead was always filled half-way up by peaks of many shapes wooded in every inch with brightest evergreens. Michoacán is celebrated for its forests.

The population showed no great difference from the peasants elsewhere. I ran early into their superstitions against photography, however, their belief, common to many uncivilized races, being that once their image is reproduced any fate that befalls it must occur to them in person. When I stepped into a field toward a man behind his wooden plow, he said in a very decided tone of voice, " No, señor, no quiero!"

" Why not? " I asked.

" Porque no quiero, señor," and he swung the sort of small adze he carried to break up the clods of the field rather loosely and with a determined gleam in his eye. I did not want the picture so badly as all that.

There was no such objection in the straggling town made of thatch and rubbish I found along the way early in the afternoon. The hut I entered for

food had an unleveled earth floor, many wide cracks
in the roof, and every inch within was black with soot
of the cooking-stove — three large stones with a
steaming earthen pot on them. There was *carne de
carnero*, tortillas and water, all for five cents. The
weak-kneed table was spread with a white cloth, there
were several awkward, *shallow*, home-made chairs,
and against the wall a large primitive sideboard
with glistening brown earthen pots and carefully
polished plates and bowls. When I had photographed the interior, la señora asked if I would take
a second picture, and raced away to another hut.
She soon returned with a very small and poor amateur print of two peons in Sunday dress. One of
them was her son, who had been killed by a falling
pine, and the simple creature fancied the magic contrivance I carried could turn this tiny likeness into
a life-size portrait.

Beyond, were more rocks and wooded mountains,
with vast seas of Indian corn stretching to pine-clad
cliffs, around the " shores " of which were dozens of
make-shift shacks for the guardians against theft
of the grain. Later I passed an enormous field of
maize, which more than a hundred Indians of both
sexes and every age that could stand on its own legs
were harvesting. It was a communal corn-field, of
which there are many in this region. They picked
the ears from the dry stalks still standing and, tossing them into baskets, heaped them up in various

parts of the field and at little temporary shanties a bit above the general level on the surrounding " coast." As I passed, the gang broke up and peons in all colors, male, female, and in embryo, went away in all directions like a scattering flock of birds.

Thus far there had been no suggestion of the reputed dangers of the road. But trouble is never far off in Mexico, since the failure of its rapidly changing governments to put down bands of marauders has given every rascal in the country the notion of being his own master. The sun was just setting when, among several groups coming and going, I heard ahead five peons, maudlin with mescal, singing and howling at the top of their voices. As they drew near, one of them said something to his companions about " armas." I fancied he was expressing some idle drunken wonder as to whether I was armed or not, and as he held a hand behind him as if it might grasp a rock, I kept a weather eye on him as we approached. Had the weapon I carried in sight been a huge six-shooter, even without cartridges, it would probably have been more effective than the toy automatic well loaded. As the group passed, howling drunkenly, a veritable giant of a fellow suddenly jumped toward me with an oath. I drew my putative weapon, and at the same moment the hand I had guessed to be full of rock appeared with an enormous revolver, shining new. With drunken flourishes the peon invited me to a duel. I kept him unostentatiously covered but continued serenely on my way. To have shown fear would have been as dangerous as for a lion-tamer in the cage with his pets. On the other hand, to have killed or seriously wounded one of the group would in all likelihood have meant at least a none-too-well housed delay of several years in my journey, for the courts of Mexico seldom admit pleas of provocation from a " gringo." The group bawled after me and finally, when I was nearly a hundred yards beyond, the fellow fired four shots in my general direction. But as his bright new weapon, like so many furnished his class by our enterprising arms factories, was made to sell rather than to shoot, and his marksmanship was distinctly tempered with mescal fumes, the four bullets harmlessly kicked up the dust at some distance on as many sides of me, with danger chiefly to the several groups of frightened peasants cowering behind all the rocks and rises of ground in the vicinity.

The dangers of the road in Mexico are chiefly from peons mixed with fire-water. When he is sober, the native's attitude verges on the over-cautious. But it is a double danger to the wandering " gringo," for the reason above mentioned, while the native who kills a foreigner not infrequently escapes with impunity, and " gun toting " is limited now among all classes of the men only by the disparity between their wealth and the price of a weapon.

As I passed on over the rise of ground ahead,

huddled groups of men, women, and children fell in
after me as if for protection from their own people. At dusk I entered Paracho with a good thirty
miles behind me. It was a quaint little town in a
lap of valley surrounded by pined hills and with the
overhanging Japanese eaves peculiar to the region.
The inhabitants were entirely peons and Indians,
none in " European " dress. The vision of being
carried into the place with a few stray bits of lead
lodged in one's anatomy was not alluring, and the
dark dirty little *cárcel* on the plaza looked equally
uninteresting.

I turned in at the " Mesón de la Providencia."
The keeper gave his attention chiefly to his little
liquor and corn shop wide-opening on the street.
There were several large rooms above, however, facing the great corral where mules and asses were
munching and arrieros had spread their straw and
blankets for the night, and in at least one of them
was not merely a wooden-floored cot but two sheets
to go with it. I bathed in the tin washbasin and
turned out redressed for a turn through the town.
It swarmed with liquor-shops. Apparently any one
with nothing else to do could set up a little drunkery
or street stand without government interference.
There was no pulque, the maguey being unknown to
the region, but bottled mescal and aguardiente de
caña amply made up for it. It seemed uncanny that
one could talk with ease to these unlettered dwellers

Fall plowing near Patzcuaro

Modern transportation along the ancient highway from Tzintzun-tzan, the former Tarascan capital

in the wilderness in the same tongue learned in a peaceful class-room of the far North. A towsled woman or child drifted now and then into the mesón shop to buy a Mexican-cent's worth of firewood. The woman who kept the shanty *fonda* down the street boasted of having lived nineteen months in California in her halcyon days, but was obliged to borrow enough of me in advance to buy the ingredients of the scanty supper she finally prepared. By eight the corral was snoring with arrieros and I ascended to my substantial couch.

A wintry cold of the highlands hung over Paracho when dawn crawled in to find me shivering under a light blanket. As I left the place behind, the sun began to peer through the crest pines of a curiously formed mountain to the east, and to rend and tear the heavy fog banks hanging over the town and valley. Peons tight-wrapped in their blankets from eyes to knees slipped noiselessly past. There was a penetrating chill in the air, the fields were covered white with what seemed to be hoar frost, and the grassy way was wet with dew as after a heavy shower.

Within half an hour the way began to rise and soon entered an immense pine forest without a sign of habitation. Tramping was delightful through what seemed a wild, untamed, and unteutonized Harz, with only the faint road and an occasional stump to show man had passed that way before. Huge birds circled majestically over the wooded hills and valleys of which the trail caught frequent brief but wide vistas.   The road would have just suited Hazlitt, for it never left off winding, both in and out through the whispering forest and in and out of itself by numberless paths, often spreading over a hundred yards of width, and rolling and pitching like a ship at sea. As in most of Mexico, wheeled traffic would here have been impossible.

By eight I could stuff my coat into my knapsack. The day's journey was short, and twice I lay an hour on a grassy knoll gazing at the birds and leisurely drifting clouds above and listening to the soft whispering of the pines.   Then an unraveled trail led gradually downward, fell in with a broad sandy " road " that descended more sharply to a still swifter cobbled way, and about me grew up a land reminiscent of Ceylon, with many frail wooden houses on either side among banana groves, fruit for sale before them, and frequent streams of clear water babbling past. But it was only half-tropical, and further down the way was lined with huge trees resembling the elm.

Uruapan was just high enough above the real tropics to be delightful.   The attitude of its people, too, was pleasing.   If not exactly friendly, they lacked that sour incommunicativeness of the higher plateau.   Very few were in modern costume and to judge from the crowd of boys that gathered round me as I wrote my notes in a plaza bench, the arrival of a white man in this largely Indian town was an event not to be slighted. There was a general air of more satisfaction with life in the languid country place where nature rewards all labor quickly and well, and where nearly all have gardens and orchards of their own to make them independent of working for others at a scanty wage.

Its plaza lies a bit higher than the rest of the town, and from it straight streets of one-story houses, all of different slope, flow gently down, to be lost a few blocks away in greenery. The roofs of tile or a long untapered shingle are not flat, as elsewhere, but with a slope for the tropical rains. Patio life is well developed. Within the blank walls of the central portion all the rooms open on sun-flooded, inner gardens and whole orchards within which pass almost all the family activities, even to veranda dining-rooms in the edge of the shade. Dense groves of banana and coffee trees surround most of the un-crowded, adobe dwellings. In the outskirts the houses are of wood, with sharp-peaked roofs, and little hovels of mud and rubbish loll in the dense-black cool shadows of the productive groves and of the immense trees that are a feature of the place. Flowers bloom everywhere, and all vegetation is of the deepest green. On every side the town dies away into domesticated jungle beyond which lie such pine forests, vast corn fields, and washed-out trails as on the way thither from Zamora.

There is not a " sight " of the slightest importance in Uruapan. But the place itself is a sight worth long travel, with its soft climate like the offspring of the wedded North and South, a balmy, gentle existence where is only occasionally felt the hard reality of life that runs beneath, when man shows himself less kindly than nature. A man offered to sell me for a song a tract bordering the river, with a " house " ready for occupancy, and had the place and all that goes with it been portable we should quickly have come to terms. For Uruapan is especially a beauty spot along the little Cupatitzio, where water clearer than that of Lake Geneva foams down through the dense vegetation and under little bridges quaint and graceful as those of Japan.

The sanitary arrangements, of course, are Mexican. Women in bands wash clothes along the shady banks, both sexes bathe their light-chocolate skins in sunny pools, there were even horses being scrubbed in the transparent stream, and below all this others dipped their drinking water. Here and there the water was led off by many little channels and overhead wooden troughs to irrigate the gardens and to run little mills and cigarette factories.

In the outskirts I passed the city slaughter-house. A low stone wall separated from the street a large corral ; with a long roof on posts, a stone floor, and a rivulet of water down through it occupying the center of the compound. The cattle, healthy, medium-sized steers worth fifteen dollars a head in this section, were lassoed around the horns and dragged under the roof, where another dexterously thrown noose bound their feet together and threw them on the stone floor. They were neither struck nor stunned in any way. When they were so placed that their throats hung over the rivulet, a butcher made one single quick thrust with a long knife near the collarbone and into the heart. Boys caught the blood in earthen bowls as it gushed forth and handed it to various women hanging over the enclosing wall. The animal gave a few agonized bellows, a few kicks, and died. Each was quickly skinned and quartered, the more unsavory portions at once peddled along the wall, and bare-headed Indians carried a bleeding quarter on their black thick hair to the hooks on either side of pack horses which boys drove off to town as they were loaded. There the population bought strips and chunks of the still almost palpitating meat, ran a string through an end of each piece, and carried it home under the glaring sun.

All this is commonplace. But the point of the scene was the quite evident *pleasure* all concerned seemed to take in the unpleasant business. Most of us eat meat, but we do not commonly find our recreation in slaughter-houses. Here whole crowds of boys, dogs, and noisy youths ran about the stone floor, fingering the still pulsating animal, mimicking its dying groans amid peals of laughter, wallowing in its ebbing blood, while fully as large an assemblage of women, girls, and small children hung over the wall in a species of ecstatic glee at the oft-repeated drama. Death, especially a bloody one, appeared to awaken a keen enjoyment, to quicken the sluggard pulse of even this rather peaceful Tarascan tribe. One could easily fancy them watching with the same ebullient joy the dying struggles of helpless human beings butchered in the same way. The killing of the trussed and fallen animal over the rivulet recalled the cutting out of the heart of human victims on the sacrificial stones amid the plaudits of the Aztec multitude and the division of the still quivering flesh among them, and the vulgar young fellows running around, knife in hand, eager for an opportunity to use them, their once white smocks smeared and spattered with blood, brought back the picture of the savage old priests of the religion of Montezuma. The scene made more comprehensible the preconquest customs of the land, as the antithesis of the drunken and excited Indian to the almost effeminate fear of the same being sober makes more clear that inexplicable piece of romance, the Conquest of Mexico.

There is less evidence of " religion " in Uruapan than in Zamora. Priests were rarely seen on the streets and the church bells were scarcely troublesome. Peons and a few of even higher rank, however, never passed the door of a church even at a dis-

tance without raising their hats. Twice during the
day I passed groups of women of the peon class
carrying in procession several framed chromo representations of Saint Quién Sabe, bearing in his arms
an imaginary Christ child, all of them wailing and
chanting a dismal dirge as they splashed along
through the dust in their bare feet.

A Tragedy: As I returned in the soft air of sunset from the clear little river boiling over its rocks,
I passed in a deep-shaded lane between towering banana, coffee, and larger trees about three feet of
Mexican in sarape and overgrown hat rooted to a
certain spot and shedding copious tears, while on the
ground beside him were the remnants of a glazed pot
and a broad patch of what had once been native fire-
water mingled with the thirsty sand. Some distance
on I heard a cry as of a hunted human being and
turned to see the pot remnants and the patch in the
self-same spot, but the hat and the three feet of
Mexican under it were speeding away down the lane
on wings of terror. But all in vain, for behind
stalked at even greater speed a Mexican mother,
gaining on him who fled, like inexorable fate, not
rapidly but all too surely.

The only train out of Uruapan leaves at an un-
earthly hour. The sun was just peering over the
horizon, as if reconnoitering for a safe entrance,
when I fought my way into a chiefly peon crowd
packed like a log-jam around a tiny window barely

waist high, behind which some unseen but plainly
Mexican being sold tickets more slowly than American justice in pursuit of the wealthy.   For a couple
of miles the way lay across a flat rich land of cornfields, pink with cosmos flowers.   Then the train began to creak and grind upward at dog-trot pace,
covering four or five times what would have been the
distance in a straight line and uncovering broad vistas of plump-formed mountains shaggy with trees,
and vast, hollowed-out valleys flooded with corn.
Soon there were endless pine forests on every hand,
with a thick, oak-like undergrowth.   A labyrinth of
loops one above another brought us to Ajambarán
and a bit of level track, with no mountains in the
landscape because we stood on the summit of them.
Little Lake Zirahuén, surrounded on all sides by sloping hills, half pine, half corn, gleamed with an emer-
ald blue.   The train half circled it, at a considerable
distance, giving several broad vistas, each lower than
the preceding, as we climbed to an animated box-car
station higher still.   From there we began to descend.   Over the divide was a decided change in the
landscape; again that dry, brown, thinly vegetated
country of most of the Mexican highlands.   Miles
before we reached the town of the same name, beautiful Lake Pátzcuaro burst on our sight through a
break in the hills to the left, and continued to glad-
den the eyes until we drew up at the station.

While the rest of the passengers repaired to the

In the church of ancient Tzintzuntzan is a "Descent from the
Cross" ascribed to Titian

Indians waiting outside the door of the priest's house in Tzintzuntzan

mule-tram, I set off afoot for the town, a steady
climb of two miles by a cobbled road, up the center
of which runs a line of large stones worn flat by generations of bare feet.   The man who baedekerized
Mexico says it is a "very difficult" trip afoot.
Perhaps it would be to him.   From the central line
of flat stones there ran out, every yard, at right
angles, lines of stones a bit smaller, the space between being filled in with small cobbles, with grass
growing between them.   The sun was powerful in
this thin atmosphere of more than seven thousand
feet elevation.   I was barely settled in the hotel when
the mule-tram arrived.

Patzcuaro is one of the laziest, drowsiest, most
delightful pimples on the earth to be found in a long
search.   It has little in common with Uruapan.
Here is not a suggestion of the tropics, but just a
large Indian village of mud and adobe houses and
neck-breaking, cobbled streets, a town older than
time, sowed on and about a hillside backed by pine-
treed peaks, with several expanses of plazas, all
grown to grass above their cobbled floors, shaded by
enormous ash-like trees with neither flowers, shrubs,
nor fountains to detract from their atmosphere of
roominess.   About them run *portales*, arcades with
pillars that seem at least to antedate Noah, and massive stone benches green with age and water-logged
with constant shade, as are also the ancient stone
sidewalks under the trees and the overhanging roofs

of one-story houses supported by carved beams. Along these wanders a chiefly peon population, soft-footed and silent, with a mien and manner that seems to murmur: "If I do not do it to-day there is to-morrow, and next week, and the week after." The place is charming; not to its inhabitants perhaps, but to us from a land where everything is distressingly new. To the man who has anything to do or a desire to do anything, Patzcuaro would be infernal; for him who has nothing to do but to do nothing, it is delightful.

Those who wish may visit crooning old churches more aged than the plays of Shakespeare. Or one may climb to " Calvary." The fanatical inhabitants, abetted by the wily priests, have named a road, " very rocky and very hilly," according to the Mexican Baedeker, leading to a knoll somewhat above the town, the " via dolorosa," and have scattered four-teen stations of plastered mud nitches along the way. From the aged, half-circular, stone bench on the summit is another of the marvelous views that abound in Mexico. It was siesta-time, and not a human being was in sight to break the spell. The knoll fell away in bushy precipitousness to the plain below. As I reached the top, two trains, bound back the way I had come, left the station two miles away, one behind the other, and for a long time both were plainly visible as they wound in and out away through the foothills, yet noiseless from here as phantoms, and no blot on the landscape, since all colors, even that of a railroad cutting, blended into the soft-brown whole.

The scene was wholly different from that about Uruapan, 1700 feet lower. There was very little green, and nothing at all of jungle; only a sun-faded brown tapestry backed by a jumble of low mountains covered with short bristling pines. Here and there a timid, thin-blue peak peered over a depression in the chain. A panoramic glance, starting from the west, showed range after range, one behind the other, to the dimmest blue distance. Swinging round the horizon, skipping the lake, the eye took in a continuous procession of hills, more properly the upper portions of mountains, losing their trees toward the east and growing more and more bare and reddish-brown, until it fell again on the doddering old town napping in its hollow down the slope. Below the abrupt face of " Calvario," the plain, with a few patches of still green corn alternating with reddish, plowed fields but for the most part humped and bumped, light wooded with scrub pine, was sprinkled with mouse-sized cattle, distinct even to their spots and markings in this marvelous, clear air of the highlands, lazily swinging their tails in summer contentment.

But the center of the picture, *the* picture, indeed, for which all the rest served as frame, was Lake Pátzcuaro. It is not beautiful, but rather inviting, enticing, mysterious for its many sandy promontories, its tongues of mountains cutting off a farther arm of the lake with the old Tarascan capital, and above all for its islands. One of these is flat, running out to sand at either end, and with something of an old town among the trees covering its slightly humped middle. Then there is Xanicho, pitched high in mound-shape, suggestive of Capri, rocky, bare, reddish-brown, and about its bottom, like a narrow band on a half-sunken Mexican hat, a long thin town of white walls and tiled roofs visible in all detail, a church towering above the rest to form the bow of the ribbon. It is strange how the human plant grows everywhere and anywhere, even on a patch of rock thrust forth out of the sea. A bit to the east and farther away lies a much smaller island of similar shape, apparently uninhabited. Farther still there stands forth from the water a bare precipitous rock topped by a castle-like building suggesting Chillon; and beyond and about are other islands of many shapes, but all flat and gray-green in tint, some so near shore as to blend with the promontories and seem part of the mainland, thereby losing their romance.

Over all the scene was a light-blue, transparent sky, flecked only with a few snow-white whisps of clouds, like bits of the ostrich plume that hung over Uruapan in the far west, and from which a soft wind tore off now and then tiny pieces that floated slowly eastward. The same breeze tempered the sunny stillness of the " Calvario," broken occasionally by the

song of a happy shepherd boy in the shrub-clad hills
and the mellow-voiced, decrepit, old church bells of
Pátzcuaro below.

Some miles away from the town, at the far end of
Lake Pátzcuaro, behind the hills, lies the ancient Indian village of Tzintzuntzan, at the time of the Conquest the residence of the chief of the Tarascans and
ruler of the kingdom of Michoacán, which was not
subdued until ten years after the fall of Mexico.   I
planned to visit it next day.   As I strolled around
the unkempt plaza grande in a darkness only augmented by a few weak electric bulbs of slight candle-
power, with scores of peons, male and female,
wrapped like half-animated mummies in their blankets, even to their noses, I fell in with a German.
He was a garrulous, self-complacent, ungraceful man
of fifty, a druggist and " doctor " in a small town far
down in Oaxaca State until revolutions began, when
he had escaped in the garb of a peon, leaving most of
his possessions behind.   Now he wandered from town
to town, hanging up his shingle a few days in each as
an oculist.   His hotel room was a museum.   None
can rival the wandering Teuton in the systematic collecting, at its lowest possible cost, of everything that
could by any stretch of the imagination ever be of
service to a traveler.   This one possessed only a
rucksack and a blanket-wrapped bundle, but in them
he carried more than the average American would be
caught in possession of in his own home.   There were

worn and greasy notebooks full of detailed information of the road, the cheapest hotels of every known town of Mexico, with the lowest possible price and the idiosyncrasies of their proprietors that might be played upon to obtain it, the exact café where the beer glasses grew tallest, the expenditures that might be avoided by a foresighted manipulation; there were shoes and slippers, sleeping garments for each degree of temperature, a cooking outfit, a bicycle-lamp with a chimney to read by, guns, gun-oil, gun-cleaners, flannel cloth to take the place of socks for tramping, vaseline to rub on the same — it would be madness to attempt a complete inventory, but he would be inventive indeed who could name anything that Teutonic pack did not contain in some abbreviated form, purchased somewhere second hand at a fourth its original cost. The German had learned that the parish priest of Tzintzuntzan wore glasses, and we parted agreed to make the trip together.

Patzcuaro is summery enough by day, but only the hardy would dress leisurely at dawn. A fog as thick as cheese, more properly a descended cloud, enveloped the place, a daily occurrence which the local authorities would have you think make it unusually healthful. An ancient cobbled road leads up and over the first rise, then degenerates to the usual Mexican *camino*, a trail twisting in and out along a chaos of rocks and broken ground. The fog hung long with us and made impossible pictures of the procession of

Tarascan Indians coming in from Tzintzuntzan with every species of red pottery, from cups to immense water-jars, in great nets on the backs of horses, asses, men, and women.   Beyond the railroad the trail picked its way, with several climbs over rocky spur-ends, along the marshy edge of the lake, which was so completely surrounded by mud and reeds that I had to leave unfulfilled my promised swim in it.   The trip was made endless by the incessant chatter of the "doctor," who rattled on in English without a break; and when I switched him to German his tongue sped still faster, though fortunately more correctly.   No wonder those become fluent linguists who can outdistance and outendure a man in his own tongue long before they have begun to learn it.

Along the way we picked up any amount of shining black obsidian, some in the form of arrow-heads and crude knives that bore out the statement that the Indians once even shaved with them.   It was nearly eleven when we sighted, down among the trees on the lake shore, the squat church tower of the once capital of Michoacán.   A native we spoke with referred to it as a " ciudad," but in everything but name it was a dead, mud-and-straw Indian village, all but its main street a collection of mud, rags, pigs, and sunshine, and no evidence of what Prescott describes as splendid ruins.   Earthquakes are not unknown, and the bells of the church, old as the conquest of Michoacán, hang in the trees before it.   Inside, an

old woman left her sweeping to pull aside the curtains of the reputed Titian, a " Descent from the
Cross," while I photographed it from the pulpit, for
which privilege the young peon sexton appeared in
time to accept a silver coin.

The German, with whom business always took pre-
cedence over pleasure, had gone to find the house of
the priest. When I reached the door of it on the
blank main street, he was sitting on a wooden bench
in the hallway with a dozen old women and peons.
We were admitted immediately after, as befitted our
high social standing. A plump little padre nearing
sixty, of the general appearance of a well-stuffed
grain sack draped in black robes, but of rather im-
pressive features — and wearing glasses — greeted
us with formality. The " doctor " drew a black case
from his pocket, went through some hocuspocus with
a small mirror, and within two minutes, though his
Spanish was little less excruciating than his English,
had proved to the startled curate that the glasses
he was wearing would have turned him stone-blind
within a month but for the rare fortune of this great
Berlin specialist's desire to visit the famous historical
capital of the Tarascans. The priest smoked cigarette after cigarette while my companion fitted another pair of crystals and tucked the dangerous ones
away in his own case — for the next victim. He did
not even venture to haggle, but paid the two dollars
demanded with the alacrity of a man who recognizes

A corner of Morelia, capital of Michoacán, and its ancient aqueduct

The spot and hour in which Maximilian was shot, with the chapel
since erected by Austria

his good fortune, and to whom a matter of a few pesos more or less is of slight importance. For were there not a score of Indians waiting outside eager to pay as well for masses, confessions, and all the rest of his own hocuspocus? There followed a social chat, well liquefied, after which we took our ceremonious leave. Once outside, I learned the distressing fact that the shape of the padre's bows had required crystals costing twelve cents, instead of the customary nine-cent ones.

The German set off in the blazing noonday at his swiftest pace. He was obliged to be back at the hotel by three, for the dinner must be paid for whether eaten or not. I fell behind, glad of the opportunity. Many groups of peons were returning now, without their loads, but maudlin and nasty tempered with the mescal for which they had exchanged them. My automatic was within easy reach. The oculist had criticized it as far too small for Mexican travel. He carried himself a revolver half the size of a rifle, and filed the ends of the bullets crosswise that they might split and spread on entering a body. In the outskirts of Pátzcuaro there came hurrying toward me a flushed and drunken peon youth with an immense rock in his hand. I reached for my weapon, but he greeted me with a respectful " Adiós! " and hurried on. Soon he was overtaken by two more youths and dragged back to where an older peon lay in the middle of the road, his head mashed with a rock until trickles of brain protruded. The event seemed to cause little excitement. A few stood at their doors gazing with a mild sort of interest at the corpse, which still lay in the road when I turned a corner above.

Mules drag the tram-car of Pátzcuaro laboriously up the three kilometers from the station to the main plaza, but gravitation serves for the down journey. When enough passengers had boarded it to set it in motion, we slid with a falsetto rumble down the cobbled road, a ragged boy leaning on the brake. Beyond the main railroad track a spur ran out on a landing-stage patched together out of old boards and rubbish. Peons were loading into an iron scow bags of cement from an American box-car far from home. Indians paddled about the lake in canoes of a hollowed log with a high pointed nose, but chopped sharp off at the poop. Their paddles were perfectly round pieces of wood, like churn-covers, on the end of long slim handles.

We were soon off for Morelia, capital of the State, across plains of cattle, with an occasional cut through the hills and a few brown ponds. At one station we passed two carloads of soldiers, westbound. They were nearly all mere boys, as usual, and like the policemen and rurales of the country struck one as unwisely entrusted with dangerous weapons. Morelia is seen afar off in the lap of a broad rolling plain, her beautiful cathedral towers high above all the rest.

It was brilliant noonday when I descended and walked the mile into town.

The birthplace of José Morelos and of Yturbide, first emperor of Mexico, sits 6200 feet above the sea and claims 37,000 inhabitants. It is warm and brown with dust. Architecturally it is Mexican, with flat roofs and none of the overhanging eaves of Pátzcuaro and Uruapan. From the " centro "— the nerve-center of the " torpid State," with two well-kept plazas, the plateresque cathedral of a pinkish stone worn faint and spotted with time, and the " seat of the powers of the State," all on the summit of a knoll — the entire town slopes gently down and quickly fades away into dirty, half-cobbled suburbs, brown and treeless, overrun with ragged, dust-tinted inhabitants, every street seeming to bring up against the low surrounding range. Its natural advantages are fully equal to those of Guadalajara, but here pulque grows and man is more torpid. All the place has a hopeless, or at least ambitionless, air, though in this splendid climate poverty has less tinge of misery and the appearance of a greater contentment with its lot. There is a local " poet's walk " that is not particularly poetic, a wild park beyond that is more so, and a great aqueduct over which sprawl enormous masses of the beautiful purple bourgainvillea. This ancient waterway resembles, but is far less striking than that of Segovia, for it runs across comparatively level ground and has only single arches of

moderate height and too polished construction, instead of the massive cyclopean work of immense
blocks of stone without mortar of its Spanish counterpart. Views and sunsets too often tempt the
traveler in Mexico, or I might mention that from a
little way out of town at the top of the road to
Mexico City, where the cathedral towers all but
reach the crest of the backing range, over which
hung the ocher and light-pink and saffron-yellow
clouds of the dying day.

The "Hotel Soledad" asserted its selectness by
the announcement: "En este hotel no se admiten
compañías de cómicos ni toreros," but the solitude
of its wooden-floored beds at least was distinctly
broken and often. The pompous, squeeze-centavo,
old landlady sat incessantly in her place near the
door between dining-room and kitchen, with a leather
handbag from which she doled out, almost with tears,
coppers for change and the keys to the larder, to the
cringing servants and conferred long with them in
whispers on how much she dared charge each guest,
according to his appearance. But at least Mexico
feeds well the traveler who is too hungry to be particular. He who will choose his dishes leads a sorry
life, for the hotels are adamant in their fare and
restaurants are almost unknown, except the dozens
of little outdoor ones about the market-places where
a white man would attract undue attention — if

nothing less curable — among the "pela'os" that make up 80 per cent. of the population.

The passengers to Acámbaro included two ladies of the fly-by-night species, who whiled away a somewhat monotonous journey by discussing the details of their profession with the admiring train-boy and drumming up trade in a coquettish pantomime. The junction town was in fiesta, and the second-class car of the evening train to Celaya was literally stacked high with peons and their multifarious bundles, and from it issued a stench like unto that of a congress of polecats. I rode seated on a brake, showers of cinders and the cold night air swirling about me until the festive natives thinned down enough to give me admittance. By that time we were drawing into Celaya, also in the throes of some bombastic celebration.

Like many another Mexican city the traveler chances into when the central plaza is bubbling with night life, light, and music, Celaya turned out rather a disappointment in the sunny commonplace of day. Its central square is a little garden, but almost all the rest of the town is a monotonous waste of square, bare, one-story houses with ugly plaster façades and no roofs — at least to be seen — each differing a bit from its neighbor in height, like a badly drawn up company of soldiers. The blazing sun and thick dust characteristic of all the high central plateau are

here in full force.   Like most Spanish things — con-
quests, history, buildings — it looked more striking
at a distance than when examined in detail.

Celaya is far-famed for its candy.   All over the
republic sounds the cry of "Cajetas de Celaya!"
Mexico shows a great liking for sweets; no block is
complete without its little stands or peregrinating
hawkers of all manner of temptations to the sweet-
toothed, ranging from squares of "fudge" in all
colors of the rainbow to barber-pole sticks a half-
yard long.   The station was surrounded with soap-
less old women, boys, and even men offering for sale
all sizes of the little wooden boxes of the chief local
product, in appearance like axle-grease, but delicious
far beyond its looks, and with vendors of everything
imaginable, to say nothing of a ragged, dirty multitude of all ages with no business there — nor anywhere else.

When I had spread out over two wooden seats of
the big, bustling El Paso Limited I was quickly reminded of the grim, business-bent, American engineer in gray hair, the unlit half of a cigar clamped
tightly between his teeth, I had caught a half-con-
scious glance of in the cab window.   One could literally *feel* his firm American hand at the throttle as
the heavy train gathered steady headway and raced
away to the eastward.   Across the car sat two handsome, solidly-knit young bull-fighters, their little
rat-tail *coletas* peering from behind their square-cut

hats. We sped steadily across the sun-flooded, dry, brown plateau, slightly rolling, its fields alternating between the dead tint of dry corn and newly plowed patches. Here for the first time were pulque producing fields of maguey, planted in long, straight, emerald-green rows.

As Irapuato for its strawberries, and Celaya for its sweets, so Querétaro is famed for its huge, cheap hats, of a sort of reed, large enough to serve as umbrellas, and for its opals. From the time he steps off the train here until he boards it again, the traveler, especially the " gringo," is incessantly pestered by men and boys offering for sale these worthless bright pebbles — genuine and otherwise. Here again are the same endless rows of one-story, stucco houses, intersecting cobbled and dust-paved streets, running to the four corners of the compass from a central plaza planted with tall, slim trees, the interwoven branches of which almost completely shade it. The cathedral houses, among other disturbing, disgusting, and positively indecent representations of the Crucifixion and various martyrdoms done in the Aztec style of bloody realism, a life-size *Cristo* with masses of long real hair and a pair of knee-length knit drawers for decency's sake. One might fancy the place weighed down by a Puritan censorship. The local museum contains among other rubbish of the past the keyhole through which Josefa whispered in 1810 the words that started the revolution against

Spanish power! Here, too, is what purports to be
an authentic photograph of the execution of Maximilian, theatrical to a Spanish degree, the three victims standing in their places, the once " Emperor of
the Mexicans " holding a large crucifix, and several
of the boy soldiers who executed them crowded
eagerly into the corners of the picture. More im-
pressive to the incredulous is the plain, tapering,
wooden coffin in which the chief body was placed, the
bottom half covered with faded blood and on one of
the sides the plain, dull-red imprint of a hand, as if
the corpse had made some post-mortem effort to rise
from the dead. The portrait of the transplanted
scion of Austria shows a haughty, I-am-of-superior-
clay man, of a distinctly mediocre grade of intellect,
with a forest of beard that strives in vain to conceal
an almost complete absence of chin.

History records that the deposed ruler reached by
carriage his last earthly scene in the early morning
of June 19, 1867. I arrived as early, though afoot.
It is a twenty-minute walk from the center of town
across the flat, fertile vega, green with gardens, to
the Cerro de las Campanas, a bare, stern, stony hill,
somewhat grown with cactus bushes, maguey, and
tough shrubs, rising perhaps seventy feet above the
level of the town. It runs up gently and evenly from
the south, but falls away abruptly in a cragged, rock
precipice on the side facing Querétaro, providing the
only place in the vicinity where poorly aimed bullets

The market of Tlaxcala, the ancient inhabitants of which aided
Cortez in the Conquest of Mexico

A *rural* of the state of Tlaxcala on guard before a barracks

cannot whistle away across the plain. Before them, as they faced the youthful, brown file of soldiers in their many-patched and faded garb, the three had a comprehensive view of the town, chiefly trees and churches sufficient to house the entire populace several times over. Nine immense structures, each with a great dome and a tower or two — steeples are unknown in Mexico — stand out against the bare, brown, flat-topped range beyond that barely rises above the highest tower. The last scene he looked on must have struck the refuted emperor as typical of a country he was sorry then ever to have seen, in spite of his regal control of facial expression,— a hard, stony plateau, the fertility and riches of which succumb chiefly to an all-devouring priesthood. Cold lead plays too large a part in the history of Mexico, but certainly its most unjust verdict was not the extinction of the " divine right " in the person of this self-styled descendant of the Cæsars at the hands of an Indian of Oaxaca. To-day a brown stone chapel, erected by Austria, stands where Maximilian fell, but the spot remains otherwise unchanged, and no doubt the fathers of these same peons who toiled now in the gardens of the vega under the morning sun lined the way through which the carriage bore to its American extinction a system foreign to the Western Hemisphere.

CHAPTER VI

THE El Paso Limited picked me up again
twenty-four hours later. Beyond Querétaro's
ungainly aqueduct spread fields of tobacco, blooming
with a flower not unlike the lily; then vast, almost
endless stretches of dead, dry corn up low heights on
either hand, and occasional fields of maguey in sol-
dierly files. At San Juan del Rio, famous for its
lariats, a dozen men and a woman stood in a row,
some forty feet from the train, holding coils of
woven-leather ropes of all sizes, but in glum and
hopeless silence, while a policeman paced back and
forth to prevent them from either canvassing the
train-windows or crying their wares. Evidently
some antinuisance crusade had invaded San Juan.

Mexico is a country of such vast vistas that a man
might easily be taken and executed by bandits within
plain sight of his friends without their being able to
lend him assistance. Nowhere can one look farther
and see nothing. Yet entire companies of marauders
might lie in wait in the many wild rocky barrancos
of this apparently level brown plain. Up and up we

194

climbed through a bare, stone-strewn land, touched here and there with the green of cactus, sometimes with long vistas of maize, which here hung dead in its half-grown youth because of the failure of the summer rains. Fields of maguey continued. The air grew preceptibly cooler as we wound back and forth, always at good speed behind the American engineer, mounting to the upper plateau surrounding the capital, not through mountains but by a vast, steadily rising world. Sometimes long, unmortared stone fences divided the landscape, more often mile after unobstructed mile of slightly undulating brown plain, tinted here and there by maguey, rolled by us into the north.

A special train of soldiers, with a carload of arms and munitions, passed on the way to head off the latest revolted " general." The newspapers of the capital appeared, some rabidly " anti-American," stopping at nothing to stir up the excitable native against alleged subtle plans of the nation to the north to rob them of their territory and national existence, the more reputable ones with sane editorials imploring all Mexicans not to make intervention " in the name of humanity and civilization " necessary. The former sold far more readily. The train wound hither and yon, as if looking for an entrance to the valley of Mexico. Unfortunately no train on either line reaches ancient Anáhuac by daylight, and my plan to enter it afoot, perhaps by the same route as

Cortez, had been frustrated. A red sun was just
sinking behind haggard peaks when we reached the
highest point of the line — 8237 feet above the sea —
with clumps and small forests of stocky oaks and half
Mexico stretching out behind us, rolling brown to
distant bare ranges backed by others growing blue
and purple to farthest distance. The scene had a
late October aspect, and a chilling, ozone-rich wind
blew. By dusk the coat I had all but thrown away
in the sweltering North was more than needed. We
paused at San Antonio, a jumble of human kennels
thrown together of old cans, scraps of lumber, mud,
stones, and cactus leaves, with huge stacks of the
charcoal, with the soot of which all the inhabitants
were covered, even to the postmaster who came in person for the mail sack. That week's issue of a frivol-
ous sheet of the capital depicted an antonino char-
coal-burner standing before his no less unwashed wife,
holding a new-born babe and crying in the slovenly
dialect of the "pela'o": "Why, it is white!
Woman, thou hast deceived me!"

At dark came Tula, ancient capital of the Toltecs,
after which night hid all the scene there might have
been, but for glimpses by the light of the train of
the great *tajo* cut through the hills to drain the
ancient valley of Anáhuac. On we sped through the
night, which if anything became a trifle warmer.
Gradually the car crowded to what would have been
suffocation had we not soon pulled in at Buena Vista

station, to fight our way through a howling pandemonium of touts, many shouting English, among
whom were the first Negroes I had seen in Mexico.

Mexico City was a great disappointment. The
hotel only a block from the cathedral and the site of
the great *teocalli* of the Aztecs, to which the German
in Pátzcuaro had directed me, differed not even in
its smells from a Clark-street lodging-house in Chicago. The entire city with its cheap restaurants and
sour smelling pulquerias uncountable, looked and
sounded like a lower eastside New York turned Spanish in tongue. Even morning light discovered nothing like the charm of the rest of Mexico, and though
I took up new lodgings en famille in aristocratic
Chapultepec Avenue, with a panorama of snow-
topped Popocatepetl and Ixtaccihuatl, her sleeping sister, and all the range seeming a bare gunshot
away, the imagination was more inclined to hark back
to the Bowery than to the great Tenochtitlan of the
days of Cortez.

In a word, the capital is much like many another
modern city, somewhat bleak, cosmopolitan of population, with strong national lines of demarkation,
and a caste system almost as fixed as that of India,
but with none of the romance the reader of Prescott,
Mme. Calderón, and the rest expects. Since anarchy
fell upon the land, even the Sunday procession of carriages of beauty in silks and jewels, and of rancheros
prancing by in thousand-dollar hats, on silver-

mounted and bejeweled saddles, has disappeared from
the life of the capital.   To-day the Mexican is not
anxious to parade his wealth, nor even to venture it
in business.   He is much more minded to bury it in
the earth, to hide it in his socks, to lay it up in the
great republic to the north, where neither presidents
corrupt nor Zapatistas break in and steal.

By day moderate clothing was comfortable, but
the night air is sharp and penetrating, and he who is
not dressed for winter will be inclined to keep moving.   Policemen and street-car employees tie a cloth
across their mouths from sunset until the morning
warms.   Ragged peons swarm, feeding, when at all,
chiefly from ambulating kitchens of as tattered hawkers.   The well-to-do Mexican, the " upper class,"
in general is a more churlish, impolite, irresponsible,
completely inefficient fellow than even the countryman and the peon, in whom, if anywhere within its
borders, lies the future hope of Mexico.   To him
outward appearance is everything, and the capital is
especially overrun with the resultant hollow baubles
of humanity.

There are a few short excursions of interest about
the capital.   Bandits have made several of them,
such as the ascent of Popocatepetl, unpopular, but a
few were still within the bounds of moderate safety.
Three miles away by highway or street-car looms
up the church of Guadalupe, the sacred city of Mex-

ico. It is a pleasing little town, recalling Puree of the Juggernaut-car by its scores of little stands for the feeding of pilgrims — at pilgrimage prices. Here are evidences of an idolatry equal to that of the Hindu. Peons knelt on the floor of the church, teaching their babies to cross themselves in the long intricate manner customary in Mexico. A side room was crowded with cheap cardboard paintings of devotees in the act of being " saved " by the Virgin of Guadalupe — here a man lying on his back in front of a train which the Virgin in the sky above has just brought to a standstill; there a child being spared by her lifting the wheel of a heavy truck about to crush it. It would be hard to imagine anything more crude either in conception or execution than these signs of gratitude. To judge by them the Virgin would make a dramatist of the first rank; there was not a picture in which the miraculous assistance came a moment too soon, never a hero of our ancient, pre-Edison melodramas appeared more exactly " in the nick of time." The famous portrait of the miraculous being herself, over the high altar, is dimly seen through thick glass. Inside the chapel under the blue and white dome pilgrims were dipping up the " blessed " water from the bubbling well and filling bottles of all possible shapes, not a few of which had originally held American and Scotch whisky, that are sold in dozens of little stands outside the temple.

These they carry home, often hundreds of miles, to " cure " the ailments of themselves or families, or to sell to others at monopoly prices.

Good electric cars speed across amazingly fertile bottom lands crisscrossed by macadam highways to Xochimilco.   Nearing it, the rugged foothills of the great mountain wall shutting in the valley begin to rise.   We skirted Pedregal, a wilderness of lava hills serving as quarry, and drew up in the old Indian town, of a charm all its own, with its hoar and rugged old church and its houses built of upright cornstalks or reeds, with roofs of grass from the lake. Indians paddled in clumsy, leaky boats about through the canals among rich, flower-burdened islands, once floating.

Another car runs out to Popotla along the old Aztec causeway by which the Spaniards retreated on that dismal night of July 2, 1520.   Now the water is gone and only a broad macadamed street remains. The spot where Alvarado made his famous pole-vault is near the Buena Vista station, but no jumping is longer necessary — except perhaps to dodge a passing trolley.   Instead of the lake of Tenochtitlan days there is the flattest of rich valleys beyond. The " Tree of the Dismal Night," a huge cypress under which Cortez is said to have wept as he watched the broken remnants of his army file past, is now hardly more than an enormous, hollow, burnedout stump, with a few huge branches that make it

A part of Puebla, looking toward the peak of Orizaba

Popocatepetl and the artificial hill of Cholula on which the Aztecs
had a famous temple, overthrown by Cortez

look at a distance like a flourishing tree still in the green prime of life. The day was rainy and a cold, raw wind blew. The better-clad classes were in overcoats, and the peons in their cotton rags wound themselves in blankets, old carpets, newspapers, anything whatever, huddling in doorways or any suggestion of shelter. Cold brings far more suffering in warm countries than in these of real winters.

The comandante of notorious old Belén prison in the capital spoke English fluently, but he did not show pleasure at my visit. An under-official led me to the flat roof, with a bird's-eye view of the miserable, rambling, old stone building. Its large patios were literally packed with peon prisoners. The life within was an almost exact replica of that on the streets of the capital, even to hawkers of sweets, fruit-vendors, and the rest, while up from them rose a decaying stench as from the steerage quarters of old transatlantic liners. Those who choose, work at their trade within as outside. By night the prisoners are herded together in hundreds from six to six in the wretched old dungeon-like rooms. Nothing apparently is prohibited, and prisoners may indulge with impunity in anything from cigarettes to adultery, for which they can get the raw materials.

The excursion out to the Ajusco range, south of the city, was on the verge of danger. Zapata hung about Cuernavaca and marauders frequently approached the very outskirts of the capital. Under our knapsacks we struck upward through the stony village where the train had set us down, and along a narrow road that soon buried itself in pine forests. A bright clear stream came tumbling sharply down, and along this we climbed. A mile or more out we picked up at a thatched hut an Indian boy of ten as burden-bearer and guide, though we continued to carry most of our own stuff and to trust largely to our own sense of direction. Above came a three-hour climb through pine-forested mountains, such as the Harz might be without the misfortune of German spick and spanness. He who starts at an elevation of 7500 feet and climbs 4000 upward in a brief space of time, with a burden on his back, knows he is mounting. Occasionally a dull-gray glimpse of the hazy valley of Mexico broke through the trees; about us was an out-of-the-way stillness, tempered only by the sound of birds. About noon the thick forest of great pine trees ceased as suddenly as if nature had drawn a dead-line about the brow of the mountain. A foot above it was nothing but stunted oak growths and tufts of bunch-grass large as the top of a palm-tree. On the flat summit, with hints through the tree-tops below of the great vale of Anáhuac, we halted to share the bulk of our burdens with the Indian boy, who had not brought his "itacate." The air was most exhilarating and clear as glass, though there was not enough of it to keep us from panting madly at each exertion. In the shade it was cold even in heavy coats; but merely to step out into the sunshine was to bask like lizards.

Our "guide" lost no time in losing us, and we started at random down the sharp face of the mountain to the valley 4000 feet almost directly below us. Suddenly a break in the trees opened out a most marvelous view of the entire valley of Mexico. Popocatepetl and Ixtaccihuatl stood out as clearly under their brilliant white mantles of new-fallen snow as if they were not sixty but one mile away, every crack and seam fully visible, and the fancied likeness of the second to a sleeping woman was from this point striking. The contrast was great between the dense green of the pine forests and the velvety, brown plain with its full, shallow lakes unplumbed fathoms below. Farther down we came out on the very break-neck brink of a vast amphitheater of hills, with "las ventanas," huge, sheer, rock cliffs shaped like great cathedral windows, an easy stone-throw away but entirely inaccessible to any but an aviator, for an unconscionable gorge carpeted with bright green tree-tops lay between. I proposed descending the face of the cliff below us, and led the way down a thousand feet or more, only to come to the absolutely sheer rock end of things where it would have taken half the afternoon to drop to the carpet of forest below.

There was nothing to do but to climb out again and skirt the brink of the canyon. In the rare air we were certain a score of times of being about to drop dead from exhaustion, yet a two-minute rest always brought full recovery. Then came a wild scramble of an hour along sheer rocks thick draped with moss that pealed off in square yards almost as often as we stepped on it, and threatened to drop us more than a half-mile to the tree-tops below. Climbing, clinging, and circling through a wilderness of undergrowth amid the vast forest of still, dense-green pines, but with such views of the valley of Mexico and the great snow-clads as to reward any possible exertion, we flanked at last the entire canyon. In the forest itself every inch of ground was carpeted with thick moss, more splendid than the weavings of any loom of man, into which the feet sank noiselessly. Everywhere the peaceful stillness was tempered only by a slight humming of the trees, and the songs of myriad birds, not a human being within screaming distance, unless some gang of bandits stalked us in the depth of the forest. More likely they were by now sodden with the aftermath of Sunday festivities, and anyway we were armed " hasta los dientes."

At length, as the day was nearing its close, we fell into what had once been a trail. It was moss-grown and wound erratically in and out among the trees, but went steadily down, very level compared to the work of the preceding hours, yet so steep we several times spread out at full length to slide a rod or more. The sun was setting when we came to the bottom of "las ventanas" only a couple thousand feet from where we had first caught sight of them hours before. Thereafter the trail moderated its pace and led us to the most beautiful thing of the day, a clear ice-cold stream at the bottom of the cliffs. We all but drank it dry. Then on out of the canyon and across a vast field of rye, back of which the great gorge stood like some immense stadium, with stalwart athletic pines filling all the seats. This is the spot where Wallace's "Fair God" burst forth upon the valley. We descended between immense walls of pines, half unseen in the dusk and framing a V-shaped bit of the vale of Anáhuac, a perfect crimson fading to rose color, culminating in the pink-tinted snow-clads above.

At dark we left the boy at his hut, on the walls of which his father had just hung the two deer of that day's hunt. There was no hope of catching the afternoon train from Cuernavaca, and we laid plans to tramp on across the valley floor to Tizapan. But Mexican procrastination sometimes has its virtues, and we were delighted to find the station crowded with those waiting for the delayed convoy that ten minutes later was bearing us cityward through the cool highland night.

I had hoped to walk from Mexico City to the capital of Honduras. That portion of the route from former Tenochtitlan to Oaxaca and the Isthmus of Tehuantepec, however, was not then a promising field for tramping by any one with any particular interest in arriving. I concluded to flank it by train. It was a chilly gray day when the little narrow-gage train bore us close by the miraculous temple of Guadalupe, with its hilltop cemetery and stone sails, and into the vast fields of maguey beyond. Peons and donkeys without number, the former close wrapped in their colored blankets, the latter looking as if they would like to be, enlivened the roads and trails. We skirted the shore of dull Lake Texcoco, once so much larger and even now only a few inches below the level of the flat plain, recalling that the Tenochtitlan of the Conquest was an island reached only by causeways. At San Juan Teotihuacan, the famous pyramids lost in the nebulous haze of pre-Toltec history bulked forth from the plain and for many miles beyond. The smaller, called that of the Moon, was a mere squat mound of earth. But the larger had lately been cleared off, and was now of a light cement color, rising in four terraces with a low monument or building on the summit. It contains about the same material as the pyramid of Cheops, but is larger at the base and by no means so high, thereby losing something of the majesty of its Egyptian counterpart.

A cheery sun appeared, but the air remained cool. Fields of maguey in mathematically straight lines stretched up and away out of sight over broad rolling ridges. I had put off the experience of tasting the product until I should reach Apam, the center of the pulque industry. At that station an old woman sold me a sort of flower-pot full of the stuff at two cents. I expected to taste and throw it away. Instead there came a regret that I had not taken to it long before. It was of the consistency and color of milk, with a suggestion of buttermilk in its taste and fully as palatable as the latter, with no noticeable evidence of intoxicating properties. No doubt this would come with age, as well as the sour stink peculiar to the pulquerías of the cities.

The train made a mighty sweep to the northward to escape from the central valley, bringing a much closer and better view of the two snow-clads, first on one, then on the farther side. By choice I should have climbed up over the " saddle " between them, as Cortez first entered the realms of Montezuma. A dingy branch line bore us off across broken country with much corn toward Puebla. On the left was a view of Malinche, famous in the story of the Conquest, its summit hidden in clouds. I was now in the Rhode Island of Mexico, the tiny State of Tlaxcala, the " Land of Corn," to the assistance from which Cortez owes his fame. The ancient state capital of the same name has been slighted by the railway and only a few decrepit mule-cars connect it with the outer world. I slighted these, and leaving my possessions in the station of Santa Ana, set off through a rolling and broken, dry and dusty, yet fertile country, with

the wind rustling weirdly through the dead brown
fields of corn. The inhabitants of the backward
little capital were even more than usually indifferent
to " gringoes," seldom giving me more than a glance
unless I asked a question, and even leaving me to
scribble my notes in peace in a shaded plaza bench.

There is nothing but its historical memories of special interest in Tlaxcala. It is a town of some 3000
inhabitants, a few hundred feet higher than Mexico
City, with many ancient buildings, mostly of stone,
often mere ruins, from the seams of surely half of
which sprout grass and flowers, as they do between
the cobbles of its streets and its large rambling plaza.
I visited the old church on the site of which Christi-
anity — of the Spanish brand — was first preached
on the American continent. Here was the same Indian realism as elsewhere in the republic. One
Cristo had " blood " pouring in a veritable river
from his side, his face was completely smeared with it,
his knees and shins were skinned and barked and covered with blood, which had even dripped on his toes ;
the elbows and other salient points were in worse condition than those of a wrestler after a championship
bout, and the body was tattooed with many strange
arabesques. There were other figures in almost as
distressing a state. A god only ordinarily maltreated could not excite the pity or interest of the
Mexican Indian, whose every-day life has its own
share of barked shins and painful adversities. It

A typical Mexican of the lowlands of Tehuantepec

A typical Mexican boy of the highlands

was amusing to find this village, hardly larger than many a one about the home of Mexican hacendados, the capital of a State. But the squads of rurales and uniformed police and the civil employees of Government were very solemn with their responsibilities. I had seen it all in an hour or two and drifted back along the five lazy miles to Santa Ana. Tlaxcala lies between two gaunt broken ridges, with rugged chains all about it, yet the little State is by no means so completely *fenced in* by nature as the imagination that has fed on Prescott pictures.

Puebla, third city of Mexico, is even colder than the capital. The snow-clads of the latter look down upon it from the west, and far away to the east stands Orizaba, highest peak of Mexico. In the haze of sunset its great mantle of new-fallen snow stood out sharply, darker streaks that ran down through the lower reaches of snow dying out in nothingness, as the mountain did itself, for as a matter of fact the latter was not visible at all, but only the snow that covered its upper heights, surrounded above, below, and on all sides by the thin gray sky of evening. By night there was music in the plaza. But how can there be life and laughter where a half-dozen blankets are incapable of keeping the promenaders comfortable? In all the frigid town there was not a single fire, except in the little d holes full of charcoal over which the place cooking. Close to my hotel was the " Casa

Serdan," its windows all broken and its stucco front
riddled with bullet holes, for it was here that two
brothers, barricading themselves against the government of Porfirio Diaz, spilled the first blood of the
long series of revolutions and worse that has followed. Already the name of the street had been
changed to " Calle de los Mártires de Noviembre,
1910."

It is nearly three hours' walk from the plaza of
Puebla to that of Cholula, the Benares of the Aztecs,
and for him who rises early it is a cold one.   What
little romance remains would have fled had I made
the trip by mule-car. As it was, I could easily
drop back mentally into the days of the Conquest,
for under the brilliant cloudless sky as I surmounted
a bit of height there lay all the historic scene before me — the vast dipping plain with the ancient
pyramid of Cholula, topped now by a white church
with towers and dome, standing boldly forth across
it, and beyond, yet seeming so close one half expected an avalanche of their snows to come down
upon the town, towering Popocatepetl and her sister,
every little vale and hollow of the " saddle " between clear as at a yard distance.   Then to the left,
Malinche and the rolling stony hills of Tlaxcala,
along which the Spaniards advanced, with the beautiful cone of Orizaba rising brilliant and clear nea
a hundred miles away.   The great rampart sep

ing them from the cherished valley must have brought
bated breath even to the hardy soldiers of Cortez.

This unsurpassed view accompanied all the rest
of the peaceful morning walk.   By nine I was climbing the great pyramid from the top of which the in-
trepid Spaniard tumbled down the ancient gods, and
about which occurred the first of the many whole-
sale massacres of Indians on the American continent.
To-day it is merely a large hill, overgrown on all
sides with grass, trees, and flowers, and with almost
nothing to bear out the tradition that it was man-
built.   From the top spreads a scene rarely surpassed.   Besides the four mountains, the ancient and
modern town of Cholula lies close below, with many
another village, especially their bulking churches,
standing forth on all sides about the rich valley,
cut up into squares and rectangles of rich-brown
corn alternating with bright green, a gaunt, low,
wall-like range cutting off the entire circle of the
horizon.   The faint music of church bells from many
a town miles away rode by on a wind with the nip
of the mountain snows in it.   But Prescott has already described the scene with a fidelity that seems
uncanny from one who never beheld it except in his
mind's eye.

To-day the pyramid is sacred to the " Virgin of
town Remedies."   Gullible pilgrims come from many
bricked around to be cured of their ills, and have
does its

left behind hundreds of doll-like figures of themselves
or the ailing limb or member made of candle wax
that breaks to bits between the fingers.   Then there
are huge candles without number, martyrs and cru-
cifixions, with all the disgusting and bloody features
of elsewhere; every kind and degree and shape and
size of fetish.   Cholula needs badly another Cortez
to tumble her gods down to the plain below and drive
out the hordes of priests that sacrifice their flocks
none the less surely, if less bloodily, than their Aztec
predecessors.

A bright red sun came up as the train swung
round to the eastward, hugging the flanks of Malinche, and rumbled away across a sandy, very
dry, but fertile country, broken by huge barrancas
or washouts, and often with maguey hedges.   Most
of my day was given up to Mr.— come to think
of it, I did not even get his name.   He drifted into
the train at the junction and introduced himself by
remarking that it was not bad weather thereabouts.
He was a tall, spare man of fifty, in a black suit
rather disarranged and a black felt hat somewhat
the worse for wear.   He carried a huge pressed-
cardboard " telescope " and wore a cane, though it
hardly seemed cold enough for one.   His language
was that of a half-schooled man, with the paucity
of vocabulary and the grammar of a ship's captain
who had left school early but had since read much
and lived more.   Whenever a noun failed him, which

Looking down on Maltrata as the train begins its descent

A residence of the Isthmus of Tehuantepec

was often, he filled in the blank with the word " proposition." Like myself, he traveled second-class because there was no fourth.

It may be that the biography which pieced itself unconsciously together as he talked needs a
sprinkle of salt here and there, but it all had the earmarks of veracity. He was a Briton, once a surgeon in the British army, with the rank of captain,
saw service with Roberts in Egypt, and was with
Kitchener at the relief of Khartum. Later he served
in India with the Scotch Grays. He looked the
part, and had, moreover, the accent and scars to go
with it. Glimpses through his conversation into the
background beyond suggested he had since been in
most parts of the world. He liked Argentina best
and the United States least, as a place of residence. Practising as a physician and oculist, he had
amassed a moderate fortune, all of which he had
lost, together with his wife and child, and possibly
a bit of his own wits, in the flood of Monterey.
Since that catastrophe he had had no other ambi-
tion than to earn enough to drift on through life.
With neither money nor instruments left, he took to
teaching English to the wealthier class of Mexicans
in various parts of the country, now in mission
schools, now as private tutor. A Methodist institution in Querétaro had dispensed with his services
because he protested against an order to make life
unpleasant to those boys who did not respond with

their spending money to a daily call for alms at the morning assembly. Six months ago he had drifted into a little town near San Marcos, wearing the title of " professor," and got together a class of private pupils, chief among them three daughters of a wealthy hacendado. Rebels came one day and in the exuberance that follows a full meal long delayed, with pulque embroidery, one of them fired two shots through the window not far from his venerable British head. The " professor " picked up a two-foot mahogany ruler, marched out into the plaza and, rapping the startled rebel over the skull, took his rifle away from him and turned it over to the delighted jefe político. From then on his future seemed assured, for if the rest of the town was poor, the hacendado's wealth was only rivaled by his daughters' longing for English.

But life is a sad proposition at best. On the Monday preceding our meeting the " professor " sat with his pupils in the shade of the broad hacienda veranda when he saw two priests wandering toward the house " like Jews with a pack of clothing to sell." " It's all up with the Swede," he told himself according to his own testimony. The prophecy proved only too true. The padres had come to order that the three daughters be god-mothers to the " Cristo " (in the form of a gaudy doll) that was to be " born " in the town on Christmas eve and paraded to the cathedral of Puebla. As their ticket

to heaven depended upon obedience, none of the faithful señoritas dreamed of declining the honor, even
though it involved the expenditure of considerable of
papá's good money and required them to spend most
of the time until Christmas rehearsing for the ceremony and "praising the glory of God" with the
priests in a room of the church, locked against
worldly intruders. Naturally this left them no time
for English. His mainstay gone, the "professor"
threw up the sponge and struck out for pastures new,
carrying his trunk-like "telescope" two hot and
sandy leagues to catch this morning train.

At Esperanza the Briton went me one better on
my own custom of "living on the country." To
the *enchiladas*, large tortillas red with pepper-sauce
and generously filled with onions, and the smaller
tortillas covered with scraps of meat and boiled egg
which we bought of the old women and boys that
flocked about the train, he added a liter of pulque.
Not far beyond, we reached Boca del Monte, the
edge of the great plateau of Mexico. A wealth of
scenery opened out. From the window was a truly
bird's-eye view of the scattered town of Maltrata,
more than two thousand feet almost directly below
in the center of a rich green valley, about the edge
of which, often on the very brink of the thick-clothed
precipice, the train wound round and round behind
the double-headed engine, traveling to every point
of the compass in its descent. The town rose up

to us at last and for the first time since mounting
to San Luís Potosí two months before, I found myself less than a mile above sea-level. Instead of
the often bare, wind-swept plateau, immense weeds
of the banana family grew up about us, and a beautiful winding vale reeking with damp vegetation
stretched before and behind us as we slid onward.
High above all else and much farther away than it
seemed, stood the majestic, snow-white peak of
Orizaba. In mid-afternoon we descended at the city
of that name.

It was large, but really a village in every feature of life. Here again were the broad eaves of
one-story, tile-roofed houses, stretching well out over
the badly cobbled streets, down the center of which
ran open sewers. The place was unkempt and unclean, with many evidences of poverty, and the air
so heavy and humid that vegetation grew even on
the roofs. I wandered about town with the "professor" while he "sized it up" as a possible scene
of his future labors, but he did not find it promising.
By night Orizaba was still well above the tropics and
the single blanket on the hotel cot proved far from
sufficient even with its brilliant red hue.

On the banks of the Coatzacoalcos, Isthmus of Tehuantepec

CHAPTER VII

TROPICAL MEXICO

IT is merely a long jump with a drop of two thousand feet from Orizaba to Córdoba. But the train takes eighteen miles of winding, squirming, and tunneling to get there. On the way is some of the finest scenery in Mexico. The route circles for miles the yawning edge of a valley dense with vegetation, banana and orange trees without number, with huts of leaves and stalks tucked away among them, myriads of flowers of every shade and color, and here and there coffee bushes festooned with their red berries. The dew falls so heavily in this region that the rank growth was visibly dripping with it.

At somnolent Córdoba I left the line to Vera Cruz for that to the southward. The car was packed with the dirty, foul-tongued wives and the children and bundles of a company of soldiers recently sent against the rebels of Juchitan. Ever since leaving Boca del Monte the day before I had been coming precipitously down out of Mexico. But there were still descents to be found, and the train raced swiftly without effort in and out through ever denser jungle, magnificent in colors, alive with birds, a land in each square yard of which the traveler feels a longing to pause and dwell for a while, to swing languidly under the trees, gazing at the snow peak of Orizaba now growing farther and farther away.

Our conveyance was a species of way-freight, which whiled away most of the day at a speed fittingly respectful to the scenery about us. With every station the population grew perceptibly more lazy. The alert, eager attitude of the plateau gave place to a languorous lethargy evident in both faces and movements. People seemed less sulky than those higher up, more communicative and approachable, but also, strangely enough, less courteous, apparently from laziness, a lack of the energy necessary for living up to the rules of that Mexican virtue. They answered readily enough, but abruptly and indifferently, and fell quickly into their customary somnolence. For a time we skirted the Río Blanco, boiling away toward the sea. Oranges were so plentiful they hung rotting on the trees. The jungle was dense, though by no means so much so as those of the Far East. On either hand were hundreds of native shacks — mongrel little huts of earth floors, transparent walls of a sort of corn-stalk, and a thick, top-heavy roof of jungle grass or banana leaves, set carelessly in bits of space chopped out of the rampant jungle. Now and then we passed gangs of men fighting back the vegetation that threatened to swallow up the track completely.

Beautiful palm-trees began to abound, perfectly round, slender stems supporting hundreds of immense leaves hanging edgewise in perfect arch shape, perhaps the most symmetrical of all nature's works. What is there about the palm-tree so romantic and pleasing to the spirits? Its whisper of perpetual summer, of perennial life, perhaps. Great luscious pineapples sold through the windows at two or three cents each. The peons of this region carried a machete in a leather scabbard, but still wore a folded blanket over one shoulder, suggesting chilly nights. The general apathy of the population began to manifest itself now in the paucity of hawkers at the stations. On the plateau the train seldom halted without being surrounded by a jostling crowd, fighting to sell their meager wares; here they either lolled in the shade of their banana groves, waiting for purchasers to come and inspect their displays of fruit, or they did not even trouble to offer anything for sale. Why should man work when his food drops year by year into his lap without even replanting? Moreover, flat noses and kinky hair were growing more and more in evidence.

Not all was jungle. As the mountains died down and faded away in the west there opened out many broad meadows in which were countless sleek cattle

tended by somnolent herdsmen on horseback.   Much
sugar-cane grew, lengths of which were sold to the
brawling soldiers' wives and the carload in general,
which was soon reeking with the juice and chewed
pulp.   By afternoon jungle was a rarity and most
of the country was a rich sort of prairie with cattle
without number, and here and there an immense tree
to break the monotony.   These rich bottomlands
that seemed capable of producing anything in un-
limited quantities were almost entirely uncultivated.
At several stations there bulked above the throng
white men in appearance like a cross between farmers
and missionaries, the older ones heavily bearded.
For a time I could not catalogue them.   Then, as
we pulled out of one town, two of what but for their
color and size I should have taken for peons raced
for the last car-step, one shouting to the other in the
strongest of Hoosier accents:

"Come on, Bud, let's jemp 'er!"

Which both did, riding some sixty feet, and dropped
off like men who had at last had their one daily excitement.   Inquiry proved that they belonged to a
colony of Mormons that has settled in several groups
in this region, where nature sets their creed a pro-
lific example.

Unbroken prairies, in their tropical form, now
stretched as far as the eye could reach, with just the
shade of a shadowy range in the far west.   The heat
had not once grown oppressive during the day.

With dusk it turned almost cold. We wound slowly on into the damp, heavy night, a faint full moon struggling to tear itself a peep-hole through the clouds, and finally at ten, seat-sore with fifteen hours of slat-bench riding, pulled up at Santa Lucrecia.

It was just such a town as dozens of others we had passed that day; a plain station building surrounded unevenly by a score or so of banana-grove huts. Here ends the railroad southward, joining that across the Isthmus of Tehuantepec. From the track of the latter a wooden sidewalk that rang drum-hollow under my heels led across a gully of unknown depth in the black night to the Hotel "El Sol Mejicano," standing-room for which had been gashed out of the jungle. It was a wooden and sheet-iron building on stilts, swarming even at night with dirty children, pigs, chickens, and yellow dogs, and presided over by a glassy-eyed, slatternly woman of French anteced-ents, the general shape of a wine-skin three-fourths full, and of a ghoulish instinct toward the purses of travelers. In one end were a dozen " rooms," sep-arated by partitions reaching half way to the sheet-iron roof, and in the other a single combination of grocery and general store, saloon and pool-table, as-sorted filth and the other attributes of outposts of civilization. The chambers were not for rent, but only the privilege of occupying one of the several beds in each. These fortunately were fairly clean, with good springs and mosquito canopies, but with only a

quilt for mattress — unless it was meant for cover —
a single sheet, and the usual two little, round, hard
mountainous pillows. Otherwise the cabins were
wholly unfurnished, even to windows. The train
that had brought us in spent the night bucking and
jolting back and forth near by; even a barefoot servant walking anywhere in the building or on the veranda set the edifice rocking as in an earthquake; two
Mexicans occupying the " room " next to my own —
more properly, the one I helped occupy — bawled
anecdotes and worse at the top of their voices most
of the night; guests were hawking and spitting and
coughing incessantly in various parts of the house;
at three a servant began beating on the door with
something in the nature of a sledge-hammer to know
if I wished to take the train Atlantic-bound, and refused to accept a negative answer; my room-mate
held the world's record for snoring; at the first suggestion of dawn every child, chicken, and assorted
animal in the building and vicinity set up its greatest
possible uproar; and I was half-frozen all night, even
under all the clothing I possessed. Except for these
few annoyances, I slept splendidly. There was at
least the satisfaction of knowing that a traveling mil-
lionaire obliged to pass a night in Santa Lucrecia
would spend it no better.

Everything was dripping wet when I fled back
across the aërial sidewalk to the station. It was not
hot, but there was a dense, heavy atmosphere in which

one felt he could be as lively and industrious as elsewhere, yet found himself dragging listlessly around
as the never-do-anything-you-don't-have-to inhabitants. Even the boyish train auditor had an irresponsible lackadaisical manner, and permitted all
sorts of petty railway misdemeanors. The child-
ishness of tropical peoples was evident on every hand.
There was no second-class car on this line, but one
third, all but empty when we started, evidently not
because most bought first-class tickets but because
the auditor was of the tropics. Endless jungle covered all the visible world, with only the line of rails
crowding through it. The cocoanut palms and those
top-heavy with what looked like enormous bunches
of dates soon died out as we left the vicinity of the
coast. At Rincon Antonio the car filled up, and
among the new-comers were many of the far-famed
women of Tehuantepec. Some were of striking
beauty, almost all were splendid physical specimens
and all had a charming and alluring smile. They
dressed very briefly — a gay square of cloth about
their limbs, carelessly tucked in at the waist, and a
sleeveless upper garment that failed to make con-
nections with the lower, recalling the women of Ceylon. The absence of any other garments was all too
evident. Almost all wore in their jet-black hair a
few red flowers, all displayed six inches or more of
silky brown skin at the waist, and the majority wore
necklaces of gold coins, generally American five and

ten dollar gold pieces. To see one of them stretched out at full length on a seat, smoking a cigarette and in animated conversation with a man that five minutes before had been a total stranger, might have suggested a certain looseness of character. But this was denied by their facial expression, which bore out the claim of a chance acquaintance long resident among them that they are very frank, " simple," and friendly, but far more apt to keep within a well-defined limit than the average of tropical women. Tehuantepec, indeed, is the land of " woman's rights." The men having been largely killed off during the days of Diaz, the feminine stock is to-day the sturdier, more intelligent, and industrious, and arrogates to itself a far greater freedom than the average Mexican woman. Many of those in the car spoke the local Indian dialect, Zapoteca, but all seemed possessed of fluent Spanish.

Yet how different was all the carload from what we have come to consider " civilized " people. If the aim of humanity is to be happy in the present, then these languid, brown races are on the right track. If that aim is to advance, develop, and accomplish, they must be classed with the lower animals.

For a half hour before reaching Rincon Antonio, we had been winding with a little brawling river through a hilly gorge dense-grown with vegetation. The town was in the lull between two revolts. A bare four days before, a former chief and his followers

Women of Tehuantepec in the market-place

On the hillside above Tehuantepec are dwellings partly dug out of the cliffs

had been taken by the populace and shot behind the water-tank beside where we paused at the station. A week later new riots were to break out. But to-day the place was sunk in its customary languor, and only a few bullet-ridden walls and charred ruins hinted its recent history.

I had pictured the Isthmus of Tehuantepec a flat neck of land from ocean to ocean. But the imagination is a deceitful guide. Beyond the town of the water-tank we wormed for miles through mountains higher than the Berkshires, resembling them indeed in form and wealth of vegetation, though with a tropical tinge. The jungle, however, died out, and the train crawled at a snail's pace, often looping back upon itself, through landscapes in which the organ-cactus was most conspicuous. Even here the great chain known as the Rockies and the Andes, that stretches from Alaska to Patagonia, imposes a considerable barrier between the two seas. There was a cosmopolitan tinge to this region, and the *boinas* of Basques mingled with the cast-iron faces of Americans and sturdy self-possessed Negroes under broad "Texas" hats. An hour beyond the hills, in a thick-wooded land, I dropped off at the town of Tehuantepec, an intangible place that I had some difficulty in definitely locating in the thickening darkness.

Here was a new kind of Mexico. In many things, besides the naked, brown waists of the women, it carried the mind back to Ceylon. There were the same reed and thatched huts, almost all surrounded by spacious yards fenced by corn-stalk walls through which the inmates could see easily but be seen with difficulty.   Here, too, boys went naked until the approach of puberty; the cocoanut palms, the dense banana groves, even the huge earthen water-jars before the houses recalled the charming isle of the Singhalese, and if the people were less kindly to the stranger they were much more joyful and full of laughter than the Mexican of the plateau.   In this perhaps they had more in common with the Burmese. The men, often almost white in color, wore few large hats, never one approaching those of the highlands. The hotter the sun, the smaller the hat, seems to be the rule in Mexico.   Here it was hot, indeed; a dense, thick, tangible heat, that if it did not sap the strength suggested the husbanding of it.

A fiesta raged on the night of my arrival.   The not too musical blare of a band drew me to a wide, inclined street paved in sand, at the blind end of which were seated five rows of women in as many gradations, and everywhere shuttled men and boys, almost all in white trousers, with a shirt of the same color, Chinese-fashion, outside it, commonly barefoot with or without sandals.   A few even wore shoes. I hesitated to join the throng.   The subconscious expectation of getting a knife or a bullet in the back grows second nature in Mexico.   Few foreigners but have contracted the habit of stepping aside to let

pass a man who hangs long at their heels.   The approach of a staggering, talkative peon was always an
occasion for alertness, and one that came holding a
hand behind him was an object of undivided curiosity
until the concealed member appeared, clutching perhaps nothing more interesting than a cigar or a
banana.   Mexicans in crowds, mixed with liquor and
" religion," were always worth attention; and here
was just such a mixture, for the fiesta was in honor
of the Virgin, and the libations that had been poured
out in her honor were generous.   But the drink of
Tehuantepec, whatever it might be — for pulque is
unknown in the tropics — appeared to make its devotees merely gay and boisterous.   The adults were
friendly, even to an American, and the children
shouted greetings to me as " Señor Gringo," which
here is merely a term of nationality and no such op-
probrious title as it has grown to be on the plateau.

A few rockets had suggested an incipient revolution while I was at supper.   Now the scene of the
festivities was enlivened by four huge set-pieces of
fireworks, each with a bell-shaped base in which a man
could ensconce himself to the waist.   One in the form
of a duck first took to human legs and capered about
the square while its network of rockets, pin-wheels,
sizzlers, twisters, cannon-like explosions, and jets of
colored fire kept the multitude surging back and forth
some twenty minutes, to the accompaniment of maudlin laughter and the dancing and screaming of chil-

dren, while the band, frankly giving up its vain attempts to produce music, gazed with all eyes and blew an unattentive, never-ending rag-time of some two strains. A monster turkey took up the celebration where the charred and disheveled duck left off, capering itself into blazing and uproarious oblivion. The finale consisted of two gigantic figures of a man and a woman, with a marvelous array of all possible lights and noises that lasted a full half-hour, while the two barefoot wearers danced back and forth bowing and careering to each other. The aftermath ran far into the night, and brought to naught my plans to make up for the sleepless night before.

Though most of the inhabitants of Tehuantepec live on earth floors in reed and grass houses, there is scarcely a sign of suffering poverty. Little Spanish is heard among them, although even the children seem quite able to speak it. Their native Indian tongue differs from the Castilian even in cadence, so that it was easy to tell which idiom was being spoken even before the words were heard. It is the chief medium of the swarming market in and about the black shadows of a roof on legs. Here the frank and self-possessed women, in their brief and simple dress, were legion. Footwear is unknown to them, and the loose, two-piece, disconnected dress was augmented, if at all, with a black lace shawl thrown over the shoulders in the, to them, chilly mornings. But the most remarkable part of the costume, of decora-

A rear-view of the remarkable head-dress of the women of Tehuantepec, and one of their decorated bowls

A woman of northern Guatemala

tive properties only, is the head-dress common to a large per cent. of the women in town. From the back of the otherwise bare head hangs to the waist an intricate contrivance of lace and ruffles, snow-white and starched stiff, the awful complications of which no mere male would be able to describe beyond the comprehensive statement that the ensemble much resembles a Comanche chief in full war regalia. Above this they carry their loads on their heads in a sort of gourd bowl decorated with flowers, and walk with a sturdy self-sufficiency that makes a veranda or bridge quake under their brown-footed tread. They are lovers of color, especially here where the Pacific breezes turn the jungle to the eastward into a gaunt, sandy, brown landscape, and such combinations as soft-red skirts and sea-blue waists, or the reverse, mingle with black shot through with long perpendicular yellow stripes. The striking beauties of many a traveler's hectic imagination were not in evidence. But then, it is nowhere customary to find a town's best selling sapotes and fish in the market-place, and at least the attractiveness ranked high compared with a similar scene in any part of the world, while cleanliness was far more popular than in the highlands to the north.

The foreigner in Mexico is often surprised at the almost impossibility of getting the entrée into its family life. American residents of high position are often intimate friends for years of Mexican men in their cafés and male gatherings, without ever stepping across their thresholds. Much of the seclusion of the Moor still holds, even half a world distant from the land of its origin. Yet his racial pseudo-courtesy leads the Mexican frequently to extend an invitation which only long experience teaches the stranger is a mere meaningless formality. On the train from Córdoba I spent considerable time in conversation with a well-to-do youth of Tehuantepec, during which I was formally invited at least a dozen times to visit him at his home. He failed to meet me at the rendezvous set, but was effusive when I ran across him in the evening round of the plaza:

"Ah, amigo mío. Muy buenas noches. Cómo 'stá uste-e-é? So delighted! I was grieved beyond measure to miss you. I live in the Calle Reforma, number 83. There you have your own house. I am going there now. Do you not wish to accompany me? I have . . ."

"Yes, I should like to look in on you for a few moments."

"Ah, I was so sorry to miss you," he went on, standing stock still. "I must give you my address and you must write me, and I you."

There followed an exchange of cards with great formality and many protestations of eternal friendship; then an effusive hand-shake and:

"Mil gracias, señor. May you have a most pleasant voyage. Thanks again. So pleased to have met

you. Adiós. May you travel well. Hasta luego.
Adiós. Que le vaya bien," and with a flip of the
hand and a wriggling of the fingers he was gone.

That evening I returned early to the " Hotel La
Perla." Its entire force was waiting for me. This
consisted of Juan, a cheery, slight fellow in a blue
undershirt and speckled cotton trousers of uncertain
age, who was waiter, chambermaid, porter, bath-boy,
sweeper, general swipe, possibly cook, and in all but
name proprietor; the nominal one being a spherical
native on the down-grade of life who never moved
twice in the same day if it could be avoided, leaving
the establishment to run itself, and accepting phleg-
matically what money it pleased Providence to send
him. The force was delighted at the pleasure of having a guest to wait upon, and stood opposite me all
through the meal, offering gems of assorted wisdom
intermingled with wide-ranging questions. I called
for an extra blanket and turned in soon after dark.
There reigned a delicious stillness that promised
ample reparation for the two nights past. Barely
had I drowsed off, however, when there intruded the
chattering of several men in the alleyway and yard
directly outside my window. " They 'll soon be
gone," I told myself, turning over. But I was over-
optimistic. The voices increased, those of women
chiming in. Louder and louder grew the uproar.
Then a banjo-like instrument struck up, accompany-
ing the most dismally mournful male voice conceiv-

able, wailing a monotonous refrain of two short lines. This increased in volume until it might be heard a mile away. Male and female choruses joined in now and then. In the snatches between, the monotonous voice wailed on, mingled with laughter and frequent disputes. I rose at last to peer out the window. In the yard were perhaps a half-hundred natives, all seated on the ground, some with their backs against the very wall of my room, nearly all smoking, and with many pots of liquor passing from hand to hand. Midnight struck, then one, then two; and with every hour the riot increased. Once or twice I drifted into a short troubled dream, to be aroused with a start by a new burst of pandemonium. Then gradually the sounds subsided almost entirely. My watch showed three o'clock. I turned over again, grateful for the few hours left . . . and in that instant, without a breath of warning, there burst out the supreme cataclysm of a band of some twenty hoarse and battered pieces in an endless, unfathomable noise, that never once paused for breath until daylight stole in at the window.

At " breakfast " I took Juan to task.

" Ah, señor," he smiled, " it is too bad. But yesterday a man died in the house next door, and his friends have come to celebrate."

" And keep the whole town awake all night? "

" Ay, señor, it is unfortunate indeed. But what would you? People will die, you know."

A station of the "Pan-American" south of Tehuantepec

An Indian boy of Guatemala on his way home from market

Sleep is plainly not indigenous to the Isthmus of Tehuantepec.

From the neighboring town of Gamboa there runs southward a railway known as the "Pan-American." Its fares are high and a freight-train behind an ancient, top-heavy engine drags a single passenger-car divided into two classes with it on its daily journey. The ticket-agent had no change, and did not know whether the end of the line was anywhere near Guatemala, though he was full of stories of the dangers to travelers in that country. A languid, good-natured crowd filled the car. We are so accustomed to think of lack of clothing as an attribute of savages that it was little short of startling to see a young lady opposite, naked to the waist but for a scanty and transparent suggestion of upper garment, read the morning newspaper and write a note with the savoir-faire of a Parisienne in her boudoir. She wore a necklace of American five-dollar gold pieces, with a pendant of twenties, the Goddess of Liberty and the date, 1898, on the visible side, and as earrings two older coins of $2.50. Nearly every woman in the car was thus decorated to some extent, always with the medallion side most in evidence, and one could see at a glance exactly how much each was worth.

In a long day's travel we covered 112 miles. At Juchitán the passengers thinned. Much of this town had recently been destroyed in the revolution, and close to the track stood a crowded cemetery with hundreds of gorged and somnolent *zopilotes*, the carrion-crow of Mexico, about it. The country was a blazing dry stretch of mesquite and rare patches of forest in a sandy soil, with huts so few that the train halted at each of them, as if to catch its breath and wipe the sweat out of its eyes. Once, toward noon, we caught a glimpse of the Pacific. But all the day there spread on either hand an arid region with bare rocky hills, a fine sand that drifted in the air, and little vegetation except the thorny mesquite. A few herds of cattle were seen, but they were as rare as the small towns of stone huts and frontiers-man aspect. The train passed the afternoon like a walker who knows he can easily reach his night's destination, and strolled leisurely into To-nolá before sunset.

Beyond the wild-west hotel lay a sweltering sand town of a few streets atrociously cobbled. We had reached the land of hammocks. Not a hut did I peep into that did not have three or four swinging lazily above the uneven earth floor. In the center of the broad, unkempt expanse that served as plaza stood an enormous *pochote*, a species of cottonwood tree, and about it drowsed a Sunday evening gathering half seen in the dim light of lanterns on the stands of hawkers. On a dark corner three men and a boy were playing a *marimba*, a frame with dried bars of wood as keys which, beaten with small wooden mallets, gave off a weird, half-mournful music that floated slowly away into the heavy hot night. The women seemed physically the equal of those of Tehuantepec, but their dress was quite different, a single loose white gown cut very low at the neck and almost without sleeves. One with a white towel on her head and hanging loosely about her shoulders looked startlingly like an Egyptian female figure that had stepped forth from the monuments of the Nile. Their brown skins were lustrous as silk, every line of their lithe bodies of a Venus-like development and they stood erect as palm-trees, or slipped by in the sand-paved night under their four-gallon American oilcans of water with a silent, sylph-like tread.

The train, like an experienced tropical traveler, started at the first peep of dawn. Tonolá marked the beginning of a new style of landscape, heralding the woodlands of Guatemala. All was now dense and richly green, not exactly jungle, but with forests of huge trees, draped with climbing vines, interlarded with vistas of fat cattle by the hundreds up to their bellies in heavy green grass, herds of which now and then brought us almost to a standstill by stampeding across the track. In contrast to the day before there were many villages, a kind of cross between the jungle towns of Siam and the sandy hamlets of our " Wild West." A number had sawmills for the mahogany said to abound in the region. Now and then a pretty lake alive with wild fowl appeared in a frame of green. There were many Negroes, and not a few

Americans among the ranchers, sawmill hands and railway employees, while John Chinaman, forbidden entrance to the country to the south, as to that north of the Rio Grande, put in a frequent appearance, as in all Mexico. It was a languorous, easy-going land, where day-before-yesterday's paper was news. The sulky stare of the Mexican plateau had completely disappeared, and in its place was much laughter and an unobtrusive friendliness, and a complete lack of obsequiousness even on the part of the peons, who elbowed their way in and out among all classes as if there were no question as to the equality of all mankind. The daily arrival of the train seemed to be the chief recreation of the populace, so that there were signs of protest if it made only a brief stop. But there was seldom cause for this complaint, for the swollen-headed old engine was still capable of so much more than the schedule required that it was forced to make a prolonged stay at almost every station to let Father Time catch up with us.

The rumor ran that those who would enter Guatemala must get permission of its consul in Tapachula. But our own representative at that town chanced to board the train at a wayside hamlet and found the papers I carried sufficient. Two fellow countrymen raced away into the place as the train drew in, and returned drenched with sweat in time to continue with our leisurely convoy. Dakin was a boyish man from the Northern States, and Ems a swarthy " Texican " to whom Span sh was more native than English, both wandering southward in quest of jobs, as stationary and locomotive engineers respectively. They rode first-class, though this did not imply wealth, but merely that Pat Cassidy was conductor. He was a burly, whole-hearted American, supporting an enormous, flaring mustache and, by his own admission, all the " busted " white men traveling between Mexico and Guatemala. While I kept the seat to which my ticket entitled me, he passed me with a look of curiosity not unmixed with a hint of scorn. When I stepped into the upholstered class to ask him a question he bellowed, " Si' down! " The inquiry answered, I rose to leave, only to be brought down again with a shout of, " Keep yer seat! " It is no fault of Cassidy's if a " gringo " covers the Pan-American on foot or seated with peons, or goes hungry and thirsty or tobaccoless on the journey; and penniless strangers are not conspicuous by their absence along this route. As a Virginia Negro at one of the stations put it succinctly, " If dey ain't black, dey 'se white."

A jungle bewilderment of vegetation grew up about us, with rich clearings for little clusters of palm-leaf huts, jungles so dense the eye could not penetrate them. Laughing women, often of strikingly attractive features, peopled every station, perfect in form as a Greek statue, and with complexions of burnished bronze. Everywhere was evidence of a constant joy in life and of a placid conviction that Providence

or some other philanthopist who had always taken
care of them always would.   Teeth were not so uni-
versally splendid as on the plateau, but the luminous,
snapping black eyes more than made up for this less
perfect feature.

Nightfall found us still rumbling lazily on and it
was nearly an hour later that we reached Mariscal
at the end of the line, four or five scattered buildings
of which two disguised themselves under the name of
hotels.   Ems and I slept — or more exactly passed
the night — on cots in one of the rooms of transparent partitions, while Dakin, who refused to accept
alms for anything so useless, spread a grass mat
among the dozen native women stretched out along
the veranda.

CHAPTER VIII

HURRYING THROUGH GUATEMALA

THE three of us were off by the time the day had definitely dawned. Ems carried a heavy suitcase, and Dakin an awkward bundle. My own modest belongings rode more easily in a rucksack. A mile walk along an unused railroad, calf-high in jungle grass, brought us to a wooden bridge across the wide but shallow Suchiate, bounding Mexico on the south. Across its plank floor and beyond ran the rails of the "Pan-American," but the trains halt at Mariscal because Guatemala, or more exactly Estrada Cabrera, does not permit them to enter his great and sovereign republic. Our own passage looked easy, but that was because of our inexperience of Central American ways. Scarcely had we set foot on the bridge when there came racing out of a palmleaf hut on the opposite shore three male ragamuffins in bare feet, shouting as they ran. One carried an antedeluvian, muzzle-loading musket, another an ancient bayonet red with rust, and the third swung threateningly what I took to be a stiff piece of telegraph wire.

"No se pasa!" screamed the three in chorus,

spreading out in skirmish line like an army ready to oppose to the death the invasion of a hostile force. " No one can pass the bridge! "

" But why not? " I asked.

" Because Guatemala does not allow it."

" Do you mean to say three caballeros with money and passports — and shoes are denied admittance to the great and famous Republic of Guatemala? "

" Not at all, señor, but you must come by boat. The Pope himself cannot cross this bridge."

It would have been unkind to throw them into the river, so we returned to a cluster of huts on the Mexican bank. Before it drowsed a half-dozen ancient and leaky boats. But here again were grave international formalities to be arranged. A Mexican official led us into one of the huts and set down laboriously in a ledger our names, professions, bachelordoms, and a mass of even more personal information.

" You are Catholic, señor," he queried with poised pen, eying me suspiciously.

" No, señor."

" Ah, Protestant," he observed, starting to set down that conclusion.

" Tampoco."

There came a hitch in proceedings. Plainly there was no precedent to follow in considering the application of so non-existent a being for permission to leave Mexico. The official smoked a cigarette pensively and idly turned over the leaves of the ledger.

Three "gringoes" on the tramp from the Mexican boundary to the railway of Guatemala

Inside the race-track at Guatemala City is a relief map of the entire country

" Será ateo," said a man behind him, swelling his chest with pride at his extraordinary intelligence.

" That does n't fill the bill either," I replied, " nor any other single word I can think of."

But the space for this particular item of information was cramped. We finally compromised on " Sin religión," and I was allowed to leave the country. A boatman tugged and poled some twenty minutes before we could scramble up the steep, jungle-grown bank beyond. At the top of it were scattered a dozen childish looking soldiers in the most unkempt and disheveled array of rags and lack thereof a cartoonist could picture. They formed in a hollow square about us and steered us toward the " comandancia," a few yards beyond. This was a thatched mud hut with a lame bench and a row of aged muskets in the shade along its wall. Another bundle of rags emerged in his most pompous, authoritative demeanor, and ordered us to open our baggage. Merely by accident I turned my rucksack face down on the bench, so there is no means of knowing whether the kodak and weapon in the front pockets of it would have been confiscated or held for ransom, had they been seen. I should be inclined to answer in the affirmative. In the hut our passports were carefully if unintelligently examined, and we were again fully catalogued. Estrada Cabrera follows with great precision the movements of foreigners within his boundaries.

In the sandy jungle town of Ayutla just beyond, two of us multiplied our wealth many times over without the least exertion. That Dakin did not also was only due to the unavoidable fact that he had no multiplicand to set over the multiplier. I threw down Mexican money to the value of $8.30 and had thrust upon me a massive roll of $150. The only drawback was that the bills had led so long and maltreated a life that their face value had to be accepted chiefly on faith, for a ten differed from a one only as one Guatemalan soldier differs from his fellows, in that each was much more tattered and torn than the other. After all there is a delicate courtesy in a government's supplying an illiterate population with illegible money; no doubt experience knows other distinguishing marks, such as the particular breeds of microbes that is accustomed to inhabit each denomination; for even inexperience could easily recognize that each was so infested. I mistake in saying this was the only drawback. There was another. The wanderer who drops into a hut for a banana and a bone-dry biscuit, washed down with a small bottle of luke-warm fizzling water, hears with a pang akin to heart-failure a languid murmur of "Four dollars, señor," in answer to his request for the bill. It is not easy to get accustomed to hearing such sums mentioned in so casual a manner.

A little narrow-gage "railway" crawls off through the jungle beyond Ayutla, but the train ran on it yesterday and to-morrow. To-day there was nothing to do but swing on our loads and strike off southward. The morning air was fresh and the eastern jungle wall threw heavy shade for a time. But that time soon came to an end and I plodded on under a sun that multiplied the load on my back by at least the monetary multiple of Guatemala. Ems and Dakin quickly demonstrated a deep dislike to tropical tramping, though both laid claim to the degree of T. T. T. conferred on " gringo " rovers in Central America. I waited for them several times in vain and finally pushed on to the sweltering, heat-pulsating town of Pahapeeta, where every hut sold bottled firewater and a diminutive box of matches cost a dollar. Grass huts tucked away in dense groves along the route were inhabited by all but naked brown people, kindly disposed, so it required no exertion, to a passing stranger. Before noon the jungle opened out upon an ankle-deep sea of sand, across which I plowed under a blazing sun that set even the bundle on my back dripping with sweat.

But at least there was a broad river on the farther side of it that looked inviting enough to reward a whole day of tramping. The place was called Vado Ancho — the " Wide Wade "; though that was no longer necessary, for the toy railroad that operated to-morrow and yesterday had brought a bridge with it. I scrambled my way along the dense-grown farther bank, and found a place to descend to a big

shady rock just fitted for a siesta after a swim.
Barely had I begun to undress, however, when three
brown and barefoot grown-up male children, partly
concealed in astounding collections of rags, two with
ancient muskets and the third with a stiff piece of
wire, tore through the bushes and surrounded me
with menacing attitudes.

" What are you doing here? " cried the least naked.

" Why the idle curiosity? "

" You are ordered to come to the comandancia."

I scrambled back up the bank and plodded across
another sand patch toward a small collection of
jungle huts, the three " soldiers " crowding close
about me and wearing the air of brave heroes who had
saved their country from a great conspiracy. Lazy
natives lay grinning in the shade as I passed. One
of the lop-shouldered, thatched huts stood on a hil-
lock above the rest. When we had sweated up to
this, a military order rang out in a cracked treble and
some twenty brown scarecrows lined up in the shade
of the eaves in a Guatemalan idea of order. About
half of them held what had once been muskets; the
others were armed with what I had hitherto taken for
lengths of pilfered telegraph wire, but which now on
closer inspection proved to be ramrods. Thus each
arm made only two armed men, whereas a bit of in-
genuity might have made each serve three or four;
by dividing the stocks and barrels, for instance.
The tatterdemalion of the treble fiercely demanded

One of the jungle-hidden ruins of Quiraguá

The last house in Guatemala, near the boundary of Honduras

my passport, while the " army " quickly degenerated into a ragged rabble loafing in the shade.

I started to lay my rucksack on the bench along the wall, but one of the fellows sprang up with a snarl and flourished his ramrod threateningly. It was evidently a *lèse militarismus* worthy of capital punishment for a civilian to pass between a pole supporting the eaves and the mud wall of the building. I was forced to stand in the blazing sunshine and claw out my papers. They were in English, but the caricature of an officer concealed his ignorance before his fellows by pretending to read them and at length gave me a surly permission to withdraw. No wonder Central America is a favorite *locale* for comic opera librettos.

I descended again to the river for a swim, but had not yet stretched out for a siesta when there came pushing through the undergrowth three more " soldiers," this time all armed with muskets.

" What's up now? "

" The colonel wants to see you in the comandancia."

" But I just saw your famous colonel."

" No, that was only the teniente."

When I reached the hilltop again, dripping with the heat of noonday, I was permitted to sit on an adobe brick in the sacred shade. The colonel was sleeping. He recovered from that tropical ailment in time, and a rumor came floating out that he was

soon to honor us with his distinguished presence.
The soldiers made frantic signs to me to rise to my
feet. Like Kingslake before the Turkish pasha, I
felt that the honor of my race and my own haughty
dignity were better served by insisting on social
equality even to a colonel, and stuck doggedly to the
adobe brick. The rumor proved a false alarm anyway. No doubt the great man had turned over in his
sleep.

By and by the lieutenant came to say the commander was in his office, and led the way there. At
the second door of the mud-and-straw building he
paused to add in an awe-struck whisper:

"Take off your hat and wait until he calls you in."

Instead I stepped toward the entrance, but the
teniente snatched at the slack of my shirt with a
gasp of terror:

"Por Diós! Take off your revolver! If the
colonel sees it . . ."

I shook him off and, marching in with martial
stride and a haughty carelessness of attitude, sat
down in the only chair in the room except that occupied by the commander, with a hearty:

"Buenas tardes, colonel."

He was a typical guatemalteco in whole trousers
and an open shirt, but of some education, for he was
writing with moderate rapidity at his homemade desk.
He also wore shoes. His manner was far more reasonable than that of his illiterate underlings, and we

were soon conversing rationally. He appeared to
know enough English to get the gist of my passport,
but handed it back with the information that I
should have official Guatemalan permission to exist
within the confines of his eighteen-for-a-dollar country.

"You carry an apparatus for the making of
photographs," he went on. "Suppose you had taken
a picture of our fortress and garrison here?"

"Gar— How's that, Señor?"

"It is the law of all countries, as you know, not
to allow the photographing of places of military importance. Even the English would arrest you if
you took a picture of Gibraltar."

It was careless of me not to have noted the striking
similarity of this stronghold to that at the entrance
to the Mediterranean. Both stand on hills.

"And where do I get this official permission?"

"Impossible."

"Yet necessary?"

But I still carried Mexican cigarettes, a luxury in
Guatemala, so we parted friends, with the manners
of a special envoy taking leave of a prime minister.
The only requirement was that I should not open my
kodak within sight of this hotbed of military importance. I all but made the fatal error of passing
between the sacred eave-post and the wall upon my
exit, but sidestepped in time to escape unscathed,
and left the great fortress behind and above me.

After all I had been far more fortunate than a fellow countryman I met later, who had had a $200 camera smashed by this same ragged " garrison."

Siesta time was past and I struck on out of town. In the last hut an old woman called out to know why I had gone down to the river, and showed some suspicion at my answer.

" There are so many countries trying to get our war plans," she explained.

A trail wide enough for single-wheeled vehicles crowded its way between jungle walls.   In the breathless, blazing sunshine the sweat passed through my rucksack and into my formal city garments beyond, carrying the color of the sack with it.   For some time no one was abroad except a dripping " gringo " and a rare cargador in barely the rags necessary to escape complete nakedness, who greeted me subserviently and gave me most of the road.   The Indians of the region were inferior in physique to those of the Mexican plateau, ragged beyond words, and far from handsome in appearance.   Their little thatched huts swarmed, however, and almost all displayed something to sell, chiefly strong native liquor in bottles that had seen long and varied service.   There was nothing to eat but oranges green in color.   The way was often strewn with hundreds of huge orange-colored ones, but they were more sour than lemons and often bitter.   A tropical downpour drove me once into the not too effective shelter of the jungle,

A woman shelling corn for my first meal in Honduras

A vista of Honduras from a hillside, to which I climbed after losing
the trail

and with sunset a drizzle set in with a promise of increase. A woodchopper had told me I could not reach my proposed destination that night, but I pressed forward at my best pace up hill and down through an all but continuous vegetation and surprised myself by stumbling soon after dark upon electric-lighted Coatepeque, the first real town of Guatemala, and not a very real one at that.

However, a burly American ran a hotel where the bill for supper and lodging was only $15, and if the partitions of my room were bare they were of mahogany, as were also the springs of the bed. The pilfering of an extra mattress softened this misfortune somewhat, and toward morning it grew cool enough to stop sweating. When I descended in the morning, Ems and Dakin were sitting over their coffee and eggs. They had paid $5 each to ride in a covered bullock cart from Vado Ancho — and be churned to a pulp.

Reunited, we pushed on in the morning shadows. Ems and Dakin divided the weight of the former's suitcase; but even after the " Texican " had thrown away two heavy books on locomotive driving, both groaned under their loads. The sun of Guatemala does not lighten the burdens of the trail. Ems had boarded the bullock cart the proud possessor of a bar of soap, but this morning he found it a powder and sprinkled it along the way. Soap is out of keeping with Guatemalan local color anyway. Dense

forests continued, but here almost all had an undergrowth of coffee bushes.   Some of the largest coffee
fincas of Guatemala lie along this road, producing
annually to hundreds of thousands in gold.   Such
prosperity was not reflected in the population and
toilers.   The natives were ragged, but friendly, every
man carrying a machete, generally in a leather scabbard, and the women almost without exception enormous loads of fruit.   They were weak, unintelligent,
pimple-faced mortals, speaking an Indian dialect and
using Spanish only with difficulty.   Ragged Indian
girls were picking coffee here and there, even more
tattered carriers lugged it in sacks and baskets to
large, cement-floored spaces near the estate houses,
where men shoveled the red berries over and over
in the sun and old women hulled them in the shade of
their huts.

Jungle trees, often immense and polished smooth
as if they had been flayed of their bark, gave us
dense cool shade, scented by countless wild flowers.
But en cambio the soft dirt road climbed and wound
and descended all but incessantly, gradually working its way higher, until we could look out now and
then over hundreds of square miles of hot country
with barely a break in all its expanse of dense, steaming vegetation.   Coffee continued, but alternated
now with the slender trees of rubber plantations, with
their long smooth leaves, and already scarred like
young warriors long inured to battle.   The road was

really only an enlarged trail, not laid out, but following the route of the first Indian who picked his way over these jungled hills. Huts were seldom lacking; poor, ragged, cheerful Indians never. In the afternoon the trail pitched headlong down and around through a rock-spilled barranco with two sheer walls of the densest jungle and forest shutting it in. Where it crossed a stream, Dakin and I found a shaded, sandy hollow scooped out behind a broad flat rock in the form of a huge bathtub of water, clearer than any adjective will describe. Ems, whose swarthy tint and strong features suggested the opposite, was the least able to endure the hardships of the road, and lay lifeless in the shade at every opportunity.

The road panted by a rocky zigzag up out of the ravine again and on over rough and hilly going. Here I fell into conversation with an Indian finca laborer, a slow, patient, ox-like fellow, to whom it had plainly never occurred to ask himself why he should live in misery and his employers in luxury. He spoke a slow and labored, yet considerable, Spanish, of which he was unable to pronounce the f or v; saying "pinca" for finca and "pale" for vale. Those of his class worked from five to five shoveling coffee or carrying it, with two hours off for breakfast and *almuerzo*, were paid one Guatemalan dollar a day, that is, a fraction over five cents in our money, and furnished two arrobas (fifty pounds) of corn and frijoles and a half-pound of salt a month. Yet there are no more trustworthy employees than these underpaid fellows. As pay-day approaches, one of these same ragged Indians is given a grain sack and a check for several thousand dollars gold and sent to the town where the finca owner does his banking, often several days' distant. The sack half filled with the ragged bills of the Republic and their customary microbes, the Indian shoulders it and tramps back across the country to the estate, stopping at night in some wayside hut and tossing the sack into a corner, perhaps to leave it for hours while he visits his friends in the vicinity. Yet though both the messenger and his hosts know the contents of his bundle, it is very rare that a single illegible *billete* disappears en route.

We plodded on into the night, but Ems could only drag at a turtle-pace, and it became evident we could not make Retalhuleu without giving him time to recuperate. The first large hut in the scattered village of Acintral gave us hospitality. It was earth-floored, with a few homemade chairs, and a bed with board floor. Though barely four feet wide, this was suggested as the resting-place of all three of us after a supper of jet-black coffee, native bread, and cheese. Dakin and I found it more than crowded, even after Ems had spread a *petate*, or grass-mat, on the ground. The room had no door, and women and girls wandered indifferently in and out of it as we undressed, one mite of barely six smoking a huge black cigar in the most business-like manner. The place was a species of saloon, like almost every hut along the road, and the shouting of the family and their thirsty townsmen seldom ceased even momentarily until after midnight.

Having occasion to be in Guatemala City that day, I rose at two and, swallowing a cup of black coffee and two raw eggs and paying a bill of $12, struck out to cover the two long leagues left to Retalhuleu in time to catch the six-o'clock train. The moon on its waning quarter had just risen, but gave little assistance during an extremely difficult tramp. All was blackest darkness except where it cast a few silvery streaks through the trees, the road a mere wild trail left by the rainy season far rougher than any plowed field, where it would have been only too easy to break a leg or sprain an ankle. Bands of dogs, barking savagely, dashed out upon me from almost every hut. Besides four small rivers with little roofed bridges, there were many narrower streams or mud-holes to wade, and between them the way twisted and stumbled up and down over innumerable hills that seemed mountains in the unfathomable darkness. When I had slipped and sprawled some two hours, a pair of Indians, the first to be found abroad, gave the distance as " dos leguas," in other words, the same as when I had started. I redoubled my speed, pausing only once to call for water where a

light flickered in a hut, and seemed to have won the
race when at the edge of the town I came to a river
that required me to strip to the waist.   As I sprinted
up the hill beyond, the sound of a departing train
drifted out of the darkness ahead and an Indian informed me that it had been scheduled to leave at five.
Fortunately I continued, for it turned out to be a
freight, and the daily passenger left at six, so that
just as the east began to turn gray I was off on the
long ride to the capital.

The train takes twelve hours to make this run of
129 miles by a three-foot gage railroad, stopping at
every cluster of huts along the way.   The third-class
coach was little more than a box-car with two rough
benches along its sides.   The passengers were unpre-
possessing; most of them ragged, all of them unclean,
generally with extremely bad teeth, much-pimpled
faces, emaciated, and of undeveloped physique, their
eyes still possessing some of the brightness but lacking the snap and glisten of those of Tehuantepec and
the plateau.   Many were chrome-yellow with fever.
Ragged officers of law and disorder were numerous,
often in bare feet, the same listless inefficiency showing in their weak, unproductive, unshaven features.
The car grew so crowded I went to sit on the platform rail, as had a half-dozen already, though large
signs on the door forbade it.

It was after noon when we reached the first important town, Esquintla.   Here the tropics ended

and the train began to climb, so slowly we could have
stepped off anywhere, the vegetation visibly changing
in character with every mile.   On the now-crowded
platform two natives alternately ordered American
beer of the train-boy, at $5 a bottle!   At Palin we
were assailed by tattered vendors of all manner of
fruit, enormous pineapples selling for sixty guatemalteco cents.   Amatitlan also swarmed with hawkers,
but this time of candy in the form of animals of every
known and imaginable species.   Thereafter we wound
round beautiful Lake Amatitlan, a dark, smooth
stretch of water, swarming with fish and bottomless,
according to my fellow platformers, flanked by sloping, green, shrub-clad banks that reflected themselves
in it.   The train crossed the middle of the lake by a
stone dyke and climbed higher and ever higher, with
splendid views of the perfect cone-shaped volcanoes
Agua and Panteleón that have gradually thrown
themselves up to be the highest in Guatemala and visible from almost every part of the republic.   It was
growing dark when the first houses of Guatemala City
appeared among the trees, and gradually and slowly
we dragged into the station.   A bare-footed policeman on the train took the names and biographies of
all on board, as another had already done at Esquintla, and we were free to crowd out into the ragged, one-story city with its languid mule-cars.

In the " Hotel Colon " opposite Guatemala's chief
theater and shouldering the president's house, which

is tailor-shop and saloon below, the daily rate was
$12. The food was more than plentiful, but would
have been an insult to the stomach of a harvest-hand,
the windowless room was musty and dirty, the walls
splashed, spotted, and torn, and the bed was by far
the worst I had occupied south of the Rio Grande,
having not only a board floor but a mattress that
seemed to be stuffed with broken and jagged rocks.
Notwithstanding all which I slept the clock round.

If there is any " sight " in Guatemala City besides
its slashing sunlight and its surrounding volcanoes,
and perhaps its swarms of Indians trotting to and
from the market on Sundays, it is the relief map of
the entire Republic inside the race-course. This is
of cement, with real water to represent the lakes and
oceans and (when it is turned on) the rivers. Every
town, railway, and trail of any importance is marked,
an aid to the vagabond that should be required by
law of every country. On it I picked out easily the
route of my further travels. The map covers a space
as large as a moderate-sized house and is seen in all
its details from the two platforms above it. Its
only apparent fault is that the mountains and volcanoes are out of all proportion in height. But exaggeration is a common Central-American failing.

The city is populous, chiefly with shoeless inhabitants, monotonously flat, few buildings for dread of
earthquake being over one story, even the national
palace and cathedral sitting low and squat. An ele-

The chief monument of the ruins of Copán

A resident of Santa Rosa, victim of the hook-worm

vation of five thousand feet gives it a pleasant June weather, but life moves with a drowsy, self-contented air. Its people are far more obliging than the average of Mexico and have little or none of the latter's sulkiness or half-insolence. Here reigns supreme Estrada Cabrera; exactly where very few know, for so great is his dislike to assassination that he jumps about incessantly from one of his one-story residences to another, perhaps, as his people assert, by underground passages, for he is seldom indeed seen in the flesh by his fond subjects. In less material manifestations he is omnipresent and few are the men who have long outlived his serious displeasure. A man of modest ability but of extremely suspicious temperament, he keeps the reins of government almost entirely in his own hands, running the country as if it were his private estate, which for some years past it virtually has been. It is a form of government not entirely unfitted to a people in the bulk utterly indifferent as to who or what rules them so they are left to loaf in their hammocks in peace, and no more capable of ruling themselves than of lifting themselves by their non-existent boot-straps. Outwardly life seems to run as smoothly as elsewhere, and the casual passer-by does not to his knowledge make the acquaintance of those reputed bands of adventurers from many climes said to carry out swiftly and efficiently every whispered command of Guatemala's invisible ruler.

On Sunday a bull-fight was perpetrated in the
plaza de toros facing the station. It was a dreary
caricature on the royal sport of Spain. The plaza
was little more than a rounded barnyard, the four
gaunt and cowardly animals with blunted horns virtually lifeless, picadors and horses were conspicuous by their absence, and the two matadors were not
even skilful butchers. A *cuadrilla* of women did the
" Suerte de Tancredo " on one another's backs — as
any one else could have on his head or in a rocking-
chair — and the only breath of excitement was when
one of the feminine *toreras* got walked on by a fear-
quaking animal vainly seeking an exit. All in all it
was an extremely poor newsboys' entertainment, a
means of collecting admissions for the privilege of
seeing to-morrow's meat prepared, the butchers skin-
ning and quartering the animals within the enclosure
in full sight of the disheveled audience.

The train mounted out of the capital with much
winding, as many as three sections of track one above
another at times, and, once over the range, fell in
with a river on its way to the Atlantic. The country grew dry and Mexican, covered with fine white
dust and grown with cactus. At Zacapa, largest
town of the line, Dakin was already at work in a ma-
chine-shop on wheels in the railroad yards, and Ems
was preparing to take charge of one of the locomo-
tives. Descending with the swift stream, we soon
plunged into thickening jungle, growing even more

dense than that of Tehuantepec, with trees, plants, and all the stationary forms of nature struggling like an immense multitude fighting for life, the smaller and more agile climbing the sturdier, the weak and unassertive trampled to death underfoot on the dank, sunless ground. We crossed the now considerable river by a three-span bridge, and entered the banana country. English-speaking Negroes became numerous, and when we pulled in at the station of Quiraguá, the collection of bamboo shanties I had expected was displaced by several new and modern bungalows on the brow of a knoll overlooking the railroad. Here was one of the great plantations of the United Fruit Company. From the veranda of the office building broad miles of banana plants stretched away to the southern mountains. Jamaican Negroes were chiefly engaged in the banana culture, and those from our Southern States did the heavier and rougher work. Their wages ran as high as a dollar gold a day, as against a Guatemalan peso for the native peons of the coffee estates in other sections. Much of the work was let out on contract. There were a number of white American employees, college-trained in some cases, and almost all extremely youthful. The heat here was tropical and heavy, the place being a bare three hundred feet above sea-level where even clothing quickly molds and rots. My fellow countrymen had found the most dangerous pastimes in this climate to be drinking liquor and eating bananas, while the mass of employees more often came to grief in the feuds between the various breeds of Negroes and with the natives.

In the morning a handcar provided with a seat and manned by two muscular Carib Negroes carried me away through the banana jungle by a private railroad. The atmosphere was thick and heavy as soured milk. A half-hour between endless walls of banana plants brought me to a palm-leaf hut, from which I splashed away on foot through a riot of wet jungle to the famous ruins of Quiraguá. Archeologists had cleared a considerable square in the wilderness, still within the holdings of the fruit company, felling many enormous trees; but the place was already half choked again with compact undergrowth. There were three immense stone pillars in a row, then two others leaning at precarious angles, while in and out through the adjacent jungle were scattered carved stones in the forms of frogs and other animals, clumsily depicted, a small calendar stone, and an immense carved rock reputed to have been a place of sacrifice. Several artificial mounds were now mere stone hills overgrown with militant vegetation, as were remnants of old stone roadways. Every stone was covered with distinct but crudely carved figures, the most prominent being that of a king with a large Roman nose but very little chin, wearing an intricate crown surmounted by a death's-head, holding a scepter in one hand and in the other what appeared to be a child spitted on a toasting fork. All was of a species of sandstone that has withstood the elements moderately well, especially if, as archeologists assert, the ruins represent a city founded some three thousand years ago. Some of the faces, however, particularly those toward the east and south from which come most of the storms, were worn almost smooth and were covered with moss and throttling vegetation. Through it all a mist that was virtually a rain fell incessantly, and ground and jungle reeked with a clinging mud and dripping water that soaked through shoes and garments.

CHAPTER IX

THE train carried me back up the river to Zacapa, desert dry and stingingly hot with noonday. Report had it that there was a good road to Jocotán by way of Chiquimula, but the difference between a " buen camino " and a mere " road " is so slight in Central America that I concluded to follow the more direct trail. The next essential was to change my wealth into Honduranean silver, chiefly in coins of one *real*, corresponding in value to an American nickel; for financial transactions were apt to be petty in the region ahead of me. In the collection I gathered among the merchants of Zacapa were silver dollars of Mexico, Salvador, Chile, and Peru, all of which stand on terms of perfect equality with the peso of Honduras, worth some forty cents. My load was heavier, as befitted an exit from even quasi-civilization. The rucksack was packed with more than fourteen pounds, not counting kodak and weapon, and for the equivalent of some thirty cents in real money I had acquired in the market of Guatemala City a hammock, more exactly a sleep-

284

ing-net, made of a species of grass by the Indians of
Cobán.

Under all this I was soon panting up through the
once cobbled village of Zacapa and across a rising
sand-patch beyond, cheered on by the parting information that the last traveler to set out on this route
had been killed a few miles from town for the $2
or so he carried. Mine would not have been any
particular burden in a level or temperate country,
but this was neither. The sun hung so close it felt
like some immense red-hot ingot swinging overhead
in a foundry. The road — and in Central America that word seldom represents anything better than
a rocky, winding trail with rarely a level yard —
sweated up and down sharp mountain faces, picking its way as best it could over a continual succes-
sion of steep lofty ridges. Even before I lost the
railway to view I was dripping wet from cap to
shoes, drops fell constantly from the end of my nose,
and my eyes stung with salt even though I plunged
my face into every stream. My American shoes had
succumbed on the tramp to Retalhuleu and the best
I had been able to do in Guatemala City was to
squander $45 for a pair of native make and chop
them down into Oxfords. These, soaked in the jungle of Quiraguá, now dried iron-stiff in the sun and
barked my feet in various places.

I had crossed four ranges and was winding along
a narrow, dense-grown valley when night began to

fall. The rumors of foul play led me to keep a hand hanging loose near my weapon, though the few natives I met seemed friendly enough. Darkness thickened and I was planning to swing my hammock among the trees when I fell upon the hut of Coronado Cordón. It was a sieve-like structure of bamboo, topped by a thick palm-leaf roof, with an outdoor mud fireplace, and crowded with dogs, pigs, and roosted fowls. Coronado himself, attired in the remnants of a pair of cotton trousers, greeted me from his hammock.

" May I pass the night with you? "

" To be sure, señor. You may sleep on this bench under the roof."

But I produced my hammock and he swung it for me from two bamboo rafters of the low projecting eaves, beside his own and that of a horseman who had also sought hospitality, where a steady breeze swept through. His wife squatted for an hour or more over the fireplace, and at length I sat down — on the ground — to black coffee, frijoles, tortillas, and a kind of Dutch cheese.

Long before morning I was too cold, even under most of the contents of my pack, to sleep soundly. It was December and the days were short for tramping. This one did not begin to break until six and I had been awake and ready since three. Coronado slept on, but his señora arose and, covering her breasts with a small apron, took to grinding corn for

I topped a ridge and caught sight at last of Santa Rosa, first town
of any size in Honduras

Soldiers of Santa Rosa eating in the market-place

tortillas. These with coffee and two eggs dropped
for a moment in hot water, after a pin-hole had been
broken in each, made up my breakfast, and brought
my bill up to nearly eleven cents.

I was off in the damp dawn. Any enumeration of
the rocky, slippery, twisting trails by which I panted
up and over perpendicular mountain ridges under
a burning sun without the shadow of a cloud, would
be wearisome. Sweat threatened to ruin even the
clothing in my bundle, it soaked even belt and hol-
ster, rusting the weapon within it, and leaving a
visible trail behind me. Once, at the careless nod
of an Indian, I strained up an all but perpendicular
slope, only to have the trail end hundreds of feet
above the river in a fading cow-path and leave me
to climb down again. Farther on it dodged from
under my feet once more and, missing a reputed
bridge, forced me to ford a chest-deep river which
all but swept me away, possessions and all, at the
first attempt.

Jocotán, on the farther bank, was a lazy, sun-
baked village the chief industry of which seemed to be
swinging in hammocks, though I did manage to run
to earth the luxury of a dish of tough meat. Co-
motán was close beyond, then came two hours
straight up to a region of pine-trees with vistas of
never-ending mountains everywhere dense-forested,
the few adobe or bamboo huts tucked in among them
being as identically alike as the inhabitants. These

were almost obsequious peons, wearing a sort of white pajamas and moderate-sized straw hats, all strangely clean. Each carried a machete, generally with a curved point, and not a few had guns. Toward evening I struck a bit of level going amid dense vegetation without a breath of air along the bank of a river that must be forded lower down, which fact I took advantage of to perpetrate a general laundering. This proved unwise, for the sun went down before the garments had dried and left me to lug on along the stream those the unexacting customs of the country did not require me to put on wet. Every hundred yards the trail went swiftly down into the stony bed of a tributary, with or without water, and clambered breathlessly out again. A barked heel had festered and made every other step painful.

It was more than an hour after dark that I sweated into the *aldea* of Chupá, so scattered that as each hut refused me lodging I had to hobble on a considerable distance to the next. The fourth or fifth refusal I declined to accept and swung my hammock under the eaves. A woman was cooking on the earth floor for several peon travelers, but treated me only with a stony silence. One of the Indians, however, who had been a soldier and was more friendly or less suspicious of " gringoes," divided with me his single tortilla and bowl of frijoles. The family slept on dried cowskins spread on the bare earth.

Food was not to be had when I folded my hammock and pushed on at daylight. One of a cluster of huts farther up was given over to a squad of "soldiers," garrisoning the frontier, and an officer who would have ranked as a vagabond in another country sold me three tortillas and a shellful of coffee saved from his rations. Another cluster of huts marked the beginning of a stiff rocky climb, beyond which I passed somewhere in a swampy stretch of uninhabited ground the invisible boundary and entered Honduras, the Land of Great Depths.

It was indeed. Soon a vast mountain covered with pine forest rose into the sky ahead and two hours of unbroken climbing brought me only to the rim of another great wooded valley scolloped out of the earth and down into which I went all but headfirst into the town of Copán. Here, as I sat in a fairly easy chair in the shaded corner of a barnyard among pigs, chickens, and turkeys while my tortillas were preparing, I got the first definite information as to the tramp before me. Tegucigalpa, the capital, was said to be fifteen days distant by mule. On foot it might prove a trifle less. But if transportation in the flesh was laborious and slow, the ease of verbal communication partly made up for it. A telegram to the capital cost me the sum total of one *real*. It should have been a real and a quarter, but the telegraph operator had no change!

Beyond the town I found with some difficulty the gate through which one must pass to visit the ancient ruins of Copán.   Once inside it, a path led through jungle and tobacco fields and came at length to a great artificial mound, originally built of cutstone, but now covered with deep grass and a splendid grove of immense trees, until in appearance only a natural hill remained.   About the foot of this, throttled by vegetation, lay scattered a score or more of carved stones, only one or two of which were particularly striking.   Summer solitude hovered over all the scene.

Back again on the " camino real " I found the going for once ideal.   The way lay almost level along a fairly wide strip of lush-green grass with only a soft-footed, eight-inch path marking the route, and heavy jungle giving unbroken shade.   Then came a hard climb, just when I had begun to hear the river and was laying plans for a drink and a swim, and the trail led me far up on the grassy brow of a mountain, from which spread a vast panorama of pine-clad world.   But the trails of Honduras are like spendthrift adventurers, struggling with might and main to gain an advantage, only wantonly to throw it away again a moment later.   This one pitched headlong down again, then climbed, then descended over and again, as if setting itself some useless task for the mere pleasure of showing its powers of endurance.   It subsided at last in the town of Santa

Christmas dinner on the road in Honduras

Several times I met the families of soldiers tramping northward
with all their possessions

Rita, the comandante of which, otherwise a pleasant enough fellow, took me for a German. It served me right for not having taken the time to shave my upper lip. He had me write my name on a slip of paper and bade me adiós with the information that if " my legs were well oiled " I could make the hacienda Jarral by nightfall.

I set a good pace along the flat, shaded, grassy lane beside the river, promising myself a swim upon sighting my destination. But the tricky trail suddenly and unexpectedly led me far up on a mountain flank and down into Jarral without again catching sight or sound of the stream. There were three or four palm-leaf huts and a large, long hacienda building, unspeakably dirty and dilapidated. The estate produced coffee, heaps of which in berry and kernel stood here and there in the dusk. The owner lived elsewhere; for which no one could blame him. I marched out along the great tile-floored veranda to mention to the stupid *mayordomo* the relationship of money and food. He referred me to a filth-encrusted woman in the cavern-like kitchen, where three soiled and bedraggled babies slept on a dirtier reed mat on the filthy earth floor, another in a hammock made of a grain sack and two pieces of rope, amid dogs, pigs, and chickens, not to mention other unpleasantnesses, including a damp dungeon atmosphere that ought early to have proved fatal to the infants. When she had sulkily agreed to prepare me tortillas, I returned to ask the way to the river. The mayordomo cried out in horror at the notion of bathing at night, pointing out that there was not even a moon, and prophesying a fatal outcome of such foolhardiness and gringo eccentricity. His appearance suggested that he had also some strong superstition against bathing by day.

I stumbled nearly a mile along to-morrow's road, stepping now and then into ankle-deep mud puddles, before reaching the stream, but a plunge into a stored-up pool of it was more than ample reward. "Supper" was ready upon my return, and by asking the price of it at once and catching the woman by surprise I was charged only a legitimate amount. When I inquired where I might swing my hammock, the enemy of bathing pointed silently upward at the rafters of the veranda. These were at least ten feet above the tiled floor and I made several ineffectual efforts before I could reach them at all, and then only succeeded in hanging my sleeping-net so that it doubled me up like a jack-knife. Rearranging it near the corner of the veranda, I managed with great effort to climb into it, but to have fallen out would have been to drop either some eight feet to the stone-flagged door or twenty into the cobbled and filthy barnyard below. The chances of this outcome were much increased by the necessity of using a piece of old rope belonging to the hacienda, and a broken arm or leg would have been pleasant indeed here in the squalid wilderness with at least a hundred miles of mule-trail to the nearest doctor.

Luckily I only fell asleep. Several men and dirtier boys, all in what had once been white garments, had curled up on bundles of dirty mats and heaps of bags all over the place, and the night was a pandemonium of their coughing, snoring, and night-maring, mingled with the hubbub of dogs, roosters, turkeys, cattle, and a porcine multitude that snuggled in among the human sleepers. The place was surrounded by wet, pine-clad mountains, and the damp night air drifting in upon me soon grew cold and penetrating.

Having had time to collect her wits, the female of the dungeon charged me a quadrupled price for a late breakfast of black coffee and pin-holed eggs, and I set off on what turned out to be a not entirely pleasant day's tramp. To begin with I had caught cold in a barked heel, causing the cords of the leg to swell and stiffen. Next I found that the rucksack had worn through where it came in contact with my back; third, the knees of the breeches I wore succumbed to the combination of sweat and the tearing of jungle grasses; fourth, the garments I carried against the day I should again enter civilization were already rumpled and stained almost beyond repair; and, fifth, but by no means last, the few American bills I carried in a secret pocket had been almost effaced by humidity and friction.   Furthermore, the " road " completely surpassed all human powers of description.   When it was not splitting into a half-dozen faint paths, any one of which was sure to fade from existence as soon as it had succeeded in leading me astray in a panting chase up some perpendicular slope, it was splashing through mud-holes or small rivers.   At the first, stream I squandered a half-hour disrobing and dressing again, only to find that some two hundred yards farther on it swung around once more across the trail. Twice it repeated that stale practical joke.   At the fourth crossing I forestalled it by marching on, carrying all but shirt and hat,— and got only sunburn and stone-bruises for my foresight, for the thing disappeared entirely.   Still farther on I attempted to save time by crossing another small river by a series of stepping-stones, reached the middle of it dry-shod, looked about for the next step, and then carefully lay down at full length, baggage and all, in the stream as the stone turned over under my feet.   But by that time I needed another bath.

An old woman of La Libertad, a collection of mud huts wedged into a little plain between jungled mountain-sides, answered my hungry query with a cheery " Cómo no! " and in due time set before me black beans and blacker coffee and a Honduranean tortilla, which are several times thicker and heavier than those of Mexico and taste not unlike a plank of dough.

A fellow-roadster behind one of my cigars

An arriero carrying a bundle of Santa Rosa cigars on his own back as he drives his similarly laden animals

Though often good-hearted enough, these children of the wilderness have no more inkling of any line between dirt and cleanliness, nor any more desire to improve their conditions, themselves, or their surroundings, which we of civilized lands think of as humanity's privilege and requirement, than the mangy yellow curs that slink in and out between their legs and among their cooking pots. I had yet to see in Honduras a house, a garment, a single possession, or person that was anything short of filthy.

As I ate, a gaunt and yellow youth arrived with a rag tied about his brow, complaining that a fever had overtaken him on a steep mountain trail and left him helpless for hours. I made use for the first time of the small medicine case I carried. Then the old woman broke in to announce that her daughter also had fever. I found a child of ten tossing on a miserable canvas cot in the mud hut before which I sat, her pulse close to the hundred mark. When I had treated her to the best of my ability, the mother stated that a friend in a neighboring hut had been suffering for more than a week with chills and fever, but that she was " embarrassed " and must not take anything that might bring that condition prematurely to a head. I prescribed not without some layman misgiving. Great astonishment spread throughout the hamlet when I refused payment for my services, and the old woman not only vociferously declined the coin I proffered for the food, but bade

me farewell with a vehement " Diós se lo pagará "—
whether in Honduranean change or not she did not
specify. The majority of the inhabitants of the
wilds of Honduras live and die without any other
medical attention than those of a rare wandering
charlatan or pill-peddler.

Beyond was a rising path through dense steaming
jungle, soon crossed by the ubiquitous river.
Across it, near a pretty waterfall, the trail climbed
up and ever up through jungle and forest, often deep
in mud and in places so steep I had to mount on all
fours, slipping back at each step like the proverbial
frog in the well. A splendid virgin forest surrounded me, thick with undergrowth, the immense
trees whispering together far above. A half-hour
up, the trail, all but effaced, was cut off by a newly
constructed rail fence tied together with vines run
through holes that had been pierced in the buttresses
of giants of the forest. There was no other route in
sight, however, and I climbed the obstruction and
sweated another half-hour upward. A vista of at
least eight heavily wooded ranges opened out behind
me, not an inch of which was not covered with dense-
green treetops. Far up near the gates of heaven I
came upon a sun-flooded sloping clearing planted
with tobacco, and found a startled peon in the shade
of a make-shift leaf hut. Instead of climbing the
hill by this private trail, I should immediately have

crossed the river again more than an hour below and continued on along it!

When he had recovered from the fright caused by so unexpected an apparition, the Indian yielded up his double-bodied gourd and made no protest when I gurgled down about half the water he had carried up the mountain for his day's thirst.   That at least was some reward for the useless climb, for there is no greater physical pleasure than drinking one's fill of clear cold water after a toilsome tropical tramp. I crashed and slid down to the river again and picked up once more the muddy path along it between dense walls of damp jungle.   It grew worse and worse, falling in with a smaller stream and leaping back and forth across it every few yards, sometimes permitting me to dodge across like a tight-rope walker on wet mossy stones, more often delaying me to remove shoes and leggings.   An hour of this and the scene changed.   A vast mountain wall rose before me, and a sharp rocky trail at times like steps cut by nature in the rock face led up and up and still forever upward.   A score of times I seemed to have reached the summit, only to find that the trail took a new turn and, gathering up its skirts, climbed away again until all hope of its ever ceasing its sweating ascent faded away.   After all it was perhaps well that only a small portion of the climb was seen at a time; like life itself, the appalling sight of all the

difficulties ahead at once might discourage the climber
from ever undertaking the task.

It was near evening when I came out in a slight
clearing on what was at last really the summit.   Vast
forests of whispering pine-trees surrounded me, and
before and behind lay an almost endless vista of
heavily wooded, tumbled mountains, on a low one of
which, near at hand but far below, could be seen the
scattered village of San Augustín.   There was still a
long hour down the opposite face of the mountain,
with thinner pine forests and the red soil showing
through here and there; not all down either, for the
trail had the confirmed habit of falling into bottomless sharp gullies every few yards and struggling out again up the steepest of banks, though the
privilege of thrusting my face into the clear mountain stream at the bottom of each made me pardon
these monotonous vagaries.   After surmounting six
or eight such mountain ranges in a day, under a sun
like ours of August quadrupled and some twenty
pounds of awkward baggage, without what could
reasonably be called food, to say nothing of festered
heels and similar petty ailments, the traveler comes
gradually by nightfall to develop a desire to spend ten
minutes under the electric fans of a " Baltimore
Lunch."

Yet with all its difficulties the day had been more
than enjoyable, wandering through endless virgin
forests swarming with strange and beautiful forms

The great military force of Esperanza compelled to draw up and face my camera

The prisoners in their chains form an interested audience across the street

of plant and bird life, with rarely a habitation or a
fellow-man to break the spell of pure, unadulterated
nature. For break it these did. As the first hut of
San Augustín intruded itself in the growing dusk
there ran unbidden through my head an ancient refrain:

"Plus je vois l'homme, plus j'aime mon chien."

Nearer the center of the collection I paused to ask
a man leaning against his mud doorway whether he
knew any one who would give me posada. The eagerness with which he offered to do so himself gave me
visions of an exorbitant bill in the morning, but it
turned out that he was merely anxious for the
"honor" of lodging a stranger. This time I slept
indoors. My host himself swung my hammock from
two of the beams in his large, single-room house
made of slats filled in with mud. Though a man of
some education, subscriber to a newspaper of Salvador and an American periodical in Spanish, and surrounded by pine forests, it seemed never to have
occurred to him to try to better his lot even to the
extent of putting in a board floor. His mixture of
knowledge and ignorance was curious. He knew
most of the biography of Edison by heart, but
thought Paris the capital of the United States and
the population of that country 700,000.

In the house the only food was tortillas, but across
the "street" meat was for sale. It proved to be

tough strips a half-inch square of sun-dried beef hanging from the rafters. I made another suggestion, but the woman replied with a smile half of amusement half of sorrow that all the chickens had died. A few beans were found, and, as I ate, several men drifted into the hut and gradually and diffidently fell to asking strange and childish questions. It is hard for those of us trained to democracy and accustomed to intercourse only with " civilized " people to realize that a bearded man of forty, with tall and muscular frame, may have only an infantile grade of intelligence, following the conversation while it is kept on the plane of an eight-year-old intellect, but incapable of grasping any real thought, and staring with the open-mouthed naïveté of a child.

Tobacco is grown about San Augustín, and every woman of the place rolls clumsy cigars and cigarettes as incessantly as those of other parts knit or sew. The wife and daughter of my host were so engaged when I returned, toiling leisurely by the light of pine splinters; for rural Honduras has not yet reached the candle stage of progress. For a half-real I bought thirty cigarettes of the size of a lead-pencil, made of the coarse leaves more fitted to cigars. The man and wife, and the child that had been stark naked ever since my arrival, at length rolled up together on a bundle of rags on the dank earth floor, the daughter of eighteen climbed a knotched stick into a cubbyhole under the roof, and when the pine splinter flickered out I was able for the first night in Honduras to get out of my knee-cramping breeches and into more comfortable sleeping garments. The festered heel gave me considerable annoyance. A bread and milk poultice would no doubt have drawn the fever out of it, but even had any such luxury been obtainable I should have applied it internally. During the night I awoke times without number. Countless curs, that were to real dogs what these people are to civilized races, howled the night hideous, as if warning the village periodically of some imaginary danger, suggested perhaps by the scent of a stranger in their midst.   Sometime in the small hours two youths, either drunk or enamored of the bedraggled señorita in the cubbyhole above, struck up a mournful, endless ballad of two unvarying lines, the one barely heard, the other screeching the eternal refrain until the night shuddered with it. All the clothing I possessed was not enough to keep me warm both above and below.

One of the chief difficulties of the road in Honduras is the impossibility of arousing the lazy inhabitants in time to prepare some suggestion of breakfast at a reasonably early hour. For to set off without eating may be to fast all the hot and laborious day. The sun was already warm when I took up the task of picking my way from among the many narrow, red, labyrinthian paths that scattered over the hill on which San Augustín reposes and radiated into the

rocky, pine-forested, tumbled mountain world surrounding it. Some one had said the trail to Santa
Rosa was easy and comparatively level. But such
words have strange meanings in Honduras. Not
once during the day did there appear a level space
ten yards in length. Hour after hour a narrow
path, one of a score in which to go astray, worn in
the whitish rock of a tumbled and irregular series of
soft sandstone ridges with thin forests of pine or
fir, clambered and sweated up and down incessantly
by slopes steeper than any stairway, until I felt like
the overworked chambermaid of a tall but elevator-
less hotel. My foot was much swollen, and to make
things worse the region was arid and waterless.
Once I came upon a straggling mud village, but
though it was half-hidden by banana and orange
groves, not even fruit could be bought. Yet a day
or two before some scoundrel had passed this way
eating oranges constantly and strewing the trail with
the tantalizing peelings; a methodical, selfish, bour-
geois fellow, who had not had the humane carelessness to drop a single fruit on all his gluttonous
journey.

When I came at last, at the bottom of a thigh-
straining descent, upon the first stream of the day,
it made up for the aridity behind, for the path had
eluded me and left me to tear through the jungle and
wade a quarter mile before I picked up the trail
again. Refreshed, I began a task before which I

Honduras, the Land of Great Depths

might have turned back had I seen it all at once. Four mortal waterless hours I toiled steeply upward, more than twenty times sure I had reached the summit, only to see the trail, like some will-o'-the-wisp, draw on ahead unattainably in a new direction. I had certainly ascended four thousand feet when I threw myself down at last among the pines of the wind-swept summit. A draught from the gourd of a passing peon gave me new life for the corresponding descent. Several of these fellow-roadsters now appeared, courteous fellows, often with black mustaches and imperial à la Napoleon III, who raised their hats and greeted me with a sing-song " Qué se vaya bien," yet seemed remarkably stupid and perhaps a trifle treacherous. At length, well on in the afternoon, the road broke through a cutting and disclosed the welcome sight of the town of Santa Rosa, its white church bulking above all else built by man; the first suggestion of civilization I had seen in Honduras.

The suggestion withered upon closer examination. The place did not know the meaning of the word hotel, there was neither restaurant, electric light, wheeled vehicles, nor any of the hundred and one things common to civilized towns of like size. After long inquiry for lodging, I was directed to a pharmacy. The connection was not apparent until I found that an American doctor occupied there a tiny room made by partitioning off with a strip of canvas

stretched on a frame a part of the public hallway to
the patio.   He was absent on his rounds; which was
fortunate, for his Cuban interpreter not merely gave
me possession of the " room " and cot, but delivered
to me the doctor's supper of potatoes, rice, an imitation of bread, and even a piece of meat, when it
arrived from a market-place kitchen.   Here I spent
Sunday, with the extreme lassitude following an extended tramp in the hungry wilderness.   The doctor
turned up in the afternoon, an imposing monument
of a man from Texas with a wild tangle of dark-
brown beard, and the soft eyes and gentle manners
of a girl.   He had spent some months in the region,
more to the advantage of the inhabitants than his
own, for disease was far more wide spread than
wealth, and the latter was extremely elusive even
where it existed.   Hookworm was the second most
common ailment, with cancer and miscarriages frequent.   The entire region he had found virtually
given over to free love.   The grasping priests made
it all but impossible for the poorer classes to marry,
and the custom had rather died out even among the
well-to-do.   All but two families of the town acknowl-
edged illegitimate children, there was not a priest
nor a youth of eighteen who had not several, and
more than one widow of Honduranean wealth and
position whose husband had long since died continued to add yearly to the population.   The padre

of San Pedro, from whose house he had just come, boasted of being the father of eighty children. All these things were common knowledge, with almost no attempt at concealment, and indeed little notion that there might be anything reprehensible in such customs. Every one did it, why should n't any one? Later experience proved these conditions, as well as nearly 90 per cent. of complete illiteracy, common to all Honduras.

The only other industry of Santa Rosa is the raising of tobacco and the making of a tolerably good cigar, famed throughout Honduras and selling here twenty for a real. Every hut and almost every shop is a cigar factory. The town is four thousand feet above sea-level, giving it a delightful, lazy, satisfied-with-life-just-as-it-is air that partly makes up for its ignorance, disease, and unmorality. The population is largely Indian, unwashed since birth, and with huge hoof-like bare feet devoid of sensation. There is also considerable Spanish blood, generally adulterated, its possessors sometimes shod and wearing nearly white cotton suits and square white straw hats. In intelligence the entire place resembles children without a child's power of imitation. Except for the snow-white church, the town is entirely one-story, with tile roofs, a ragged flowery plaza, and straight streets, sometimes cobbled, that run off down hill, for the place is built on a meadowy knoll with a fine vista of hills and surrounded by an immensely rich land that would grow almost anything in abundance with a minimum of cultivation.

The one way of getting an early start in Honduras is to make your purchases the night before and eat them raw in the morning.   Christmas day had barely dawned, therefore, when I began losing my way among the undulating white rock paths beyond Santa Rosa.   Such a country brings home to man his helplessness and unimportance before untamed nature.   I wished to be in Tegucigalpa, two hundred miles away, within five days; yet all the wealth of Crœsus could not have brought me there in that time. As it was, I had broken the mule-back record, and many is the animal that succumbs to the up and down trails of Honduras.   This one might, were such triteness permissible, have been most succinctly characterized by a well-known description of war. It was rougher than any stone-quarry pitched at impossible angles, and the attraction of gravity for my burden passed belief.   To this I had been forced to add not merely a roll of silver reales but my Christmas dinner, built up about the nucleus of a can of what announced itself outwardly as pork and beans.   Talgua, at eleven, did not seem the fitting scene for so solemn a ceremony, and I hobbled on, first over a tumble-down stone bridge, then by a hammock-bridge to which one climbed high above the river by a notched stick and of which two thirds of the cross-

A corner of Tegucigalpa

The "West Pointers" of Honduras in their barracks, a part of the
national palace

slats were missing, while the rest cracked or broke under the 185 pounds to which I subjected them.

I promised myself to pitch camp at the very next clear stream. But the hammock-bridge once passed there began a heart-breaking climb into bone-dry hills, rolling with broken stones, and palpitating with the heat of an unshaded tropical sun. Several times I had perished of thirst before I came to a small sluggish stream, only to find its water deep blue with some pollution. In the end I was forced to overlook this drawback and, finding a sort of natural bathtub among the blazing rocks, fell upon what after all proved to be a porkless feast. The doctor's treatment had reduced the swelling in foot and ankle, but the wound itself was more painful than ever and called for frequent soaking. In midafternoon I passed a second village, as somnolent as the belly-gorged zopilotes that half-jumped, half-flew sluggishly out of the way as I advanced. Here was a bit of fairly flat and shaded going, with another precarious hammock-bridge, then an endless woods with occasional sharp stony descents to some brawling but most welcome stream, with stepping-stones or without. Thus far I had seen barely a human being all the day, but as the shades of evening grew I passed several groups of arrieros who blasted my hopes of reaching Gracias that night, but who informed me that just beyond the " rio grande " was a *casita* where I might spend the night.

It was sunset when I came to the " great river," a broad and noisy though only waist-deep stream with two sheer, yet pine-clad rock cliffs more striking than the Palisades of the Hudson. A crescent moon was peering over them when I passed the swinging bridge swaying giddily to and fro high above the stream, but on the steep farther bank it lighted up only a cruel disappointment. For the " casita " was nothing but a roof on wabbly legs, a public rest-house where I might swing my hammock but go famished to bed. I pushed on in quest of a more human habitation. The " road " consisted of a dozen paths shining white in the moonlight and weaving in and out among each other. No sign of man appeared, and my foot protested vehemently. I concluded to be satisfied with water to drink and let hunger feed upon itself. But now it was needed, not a trickle appeared. Once I fancied I heard a stream babbling below and tore my way through the jungle down a sharp slope, but I had only caught the echo of the distant river. It was well on into the night when the welcome sound again struck my ear. This time it was real, and I fought my way down through clutching undergrowth and stone heaps to a stream, sluggish and blue in color, but welcome for all that, to swing my hammock among stone heaps from two elastic saplings, for it was just my luck to have found the one spot in Honduras where there were no trees large enough to furnish shelter. Luckily nothing worse than a

heavy dew fell. Now and then noisy boisterous
bands of natives passed along the trail from their
Christmas festivities in the town ahead. But
whereas a Mexican highway at this hour would have
been overrun with drunken peons more or less dangerous to "gringoes," drink seemed to have made
these chiefly amorous. Still I took good care to ar-
range myself for the night quietly, if only to be able
to sleep undisturbed. Once, somewhere in the dark-
est hours, a drove of cattle stampeded down the slope
near me, but even as I reached for my weapon I
found it was not the band of peons from a dream of
which I had awakened. The spot was some 1500 feet
lower than Santa Rosa, but still so sharp and penetrating is the chill of night in this region in contrast
to the blazing, sweating days that I did not sleep a
moment soundly after the first hour of evening.

An hour's walk next morning brought me to
Gracias, a slovenly, nothing-to-do-but-stare hamlet
of a few hundred inhabitants. After I had eaten all
the chief hut could supply, I set about looking for the
shoemaker my already aged Guatemalan Oxfords
needed so badly. I found the huts where several of
them lived, but not where any of them worked. The
first replied from his hammock that he was sick, the
second had gone to Tegucigalpa, the third was
"somewhere about town if you have the patience to
wait." Which I did for an hour or more, and was
rewarded with his turning up to inform me that he

was not planning to begin his labors again so soon, for only yesterday had been Christmas.

Over the first hill and river beyond, I fell in with a woman who carried on an unbroken conversation as well as a load on her head, from the time she accepted the first cigar until we had waded the thigh-deep " rio grande " and climbed the rocky bank to her hut and garden.   At first she had baldly refused to allow her picture to be taken.   But so weak-willed are these people of Honduras that a white man of patience can in time force them to do his bidding by sheer force of will, by merely looking long and fixedly at them.   Many the " gringo " who has misused this power in Central America.   Before we reached her home she had not only posed but insisted on my stopping to photograph her with her children " dressed up " as befitted so extraordinary an occasion.   Her garden was unusually well supplied with fruit and vegetables, and the rice boiled in milk she served was the most savory dish I had tasted in Honduras.   She refused payment, but insisted on my waiting until the muleteers she had charged for their less sumptuous dinner were gone, so they should not discover her unpatriotic favoritism.

During the afternoon there was for a time almost level going, grassy and soft, across gently dipping meadows on which I left both mule-trains and pedestrians behind.   Houses were rare, and the fall of night threatened to leave me alone among vast

View of Tegucigalpa from the top of Picacho

Repairing the highway from Tegucigalpa to the coast

whining pine forests where the air was already chill.
In the dusk, however, I came upon the hut of Pablo
Morales and bespoke posada.   He growled a surly
permission and addressed hardly a word to me for
hours thereafter.   The place was the most filthy,
quarrelsome, pig and chicken overrun stop on the
trip, and when at last I prepared to swing my hammock inside the hut the sulky host informed me that
he only permitted travelers the corredor.   Two other
guests — ragged, soil-encrusted arrieros — were already housed within, but there were at least some advantages in swinging my own net outside from the
rafters of the eaves.   Pigs jolted against me now and
then and before I had entirely fallen asleep I was dis-
turbed by a procession of dirty urchins, each carrying a blazing pine stick, who came one by one to look
me over.   I was just settling down again when Pablo
himself appeared, an uncanny figure in the dancing
light of his flaming torch.   He had heard that I
could " put people on paper," and would I put his
wife on paper in return for his kindness in giving me
posada?   Yes, in the morning.   Why couldn't I do
it now?   He seemed strangely eager, for a man accustomed to set mañana as his own time of action.
His surly indifference had changed to an annoying
solicitude, and he forced upon me first a steaming
tortilla, then a native beverage, and finally came with
a large cloth hammock in which I passed the night
more comfortably than in my own open-work net.

In the morning heavy mountain clouds and a swirling mist made photography impossible, but my host was not of the grade of intelligence that made this simple explanation possible. He led the way into the windowless hut, in a corner of which lay a woman of perhaps thirty in a dog-litter of a bed enclosed by curtains hung from the rafters. The walls were black with coagulated smoke. The woman, yellow and emaciated with months of fever, groaned distressingly as the curtains were drawn aside, but her solicitous husband insisted on propping her up in bed and holding her with an arm about the shoulders while I " put them both on paper." His purpose, it turned out, was to send the picture to the shrine of " la Virgen de los Remedios " that she might cure the groaning wife of her ailment, and he insisted that it must show " bed and all and the color of her face " that the Virgin might know what was required of her. I went through the motions of taking a photograph and explained as well as was possible why it could not be delivered at once, with the added information to soften his coming disappointment that the machine sometimes failed. The fellow merely gathered the notion that I was but a sorry magician at best, who had my diabolical hocuspocus only imperfectly under control, and he did not entirely succeed in keeping his sneers invisible. I offered quinine and such other medicines as were to be found in my traveling case, but he had no faith in worldly remedies.

A family of Honduras

Approaching Sabana Grande, the first night's stop on the tramp to the coast

By nine the day was brilliant. There was an unusual amount of level grassy trail, though steep slopes were not lacking. During the morning I passed several bands of ragged soldiers meandering northward in rout order and some distance behind them their bedraggled women and children, all afoot and carrying their entire possessions on their heads and backs. Frequently a little wooden cross or a heap of stones showed where some traveler had fallen by the wayside, perhaps at the hands of his fellowman; for the murder rate, thanks largely to drink and vendettas, is high in Honduras. It might be less if assassins faced the death penalty, instead of being merely shut within prisons from which an active man could soon dig his way to freedom with a pocketknife, if he did not have the patience to wait a few months until a new revolution brought him release or pardon.

The futility of Honduranean life was illustrated here and there. On some vast hillside capable of producing food for a multitude the eye made out a single *milpa*, or tiny corn-field, fenced off with huge slabs of mahogany worth easily ten times all the corn the patch could produce in a lifetime — or rather, worth nothing whatever, for a thing is valuable only where it is in demand. At ten I lost the way, found it again, and began an endless, rock-strewn climb upward through pines, tacking more times than I could count, each leg of the ascent a toilsome journey in

itself. Not the least painful of road experiences in
Honduras is to reach the summit of such a range
after hours of heavy labor, to take perhaps a dozen
steps along the top of the ridge, and then find the
trail pitching headlong down again into a bottomless
gorge, from which comes up the joyous sound of a
mountain stream that draws the thirsty traveler on
at double speed, only to bring him at last to a rude
bridge over a precipitous, rock-sided river impossible
to reach before attacking the next slope staring him
in the face.

Luckily I foraged an imitation dinner in San Juan,
a scattering of mud huts on a broad upland plain,
most of the adult inhabitants of which were away
at some work or play in the surrounding hills.
Cattle without number dotted the patches of unlevel
meadows, but not a drop of milk was to be had.
Roosters would have made the night a torture, yet
three eggs rewarded the canvassing of the entire
hamlet. These it is always the Honduranean custom to puncture with a small hole before dropping
into hot water, no doubt because there was no other
way of getting the universal uncleanliness into them.
Nor did I ever succeed in getting them more than
half cooked. Once I offered an old woman an extra
real if she would boil them a full three minutes without puncturing them. She asserted that without a
hole in the end " the water could not get in to cook
them," but at length solemnly promised to follow my

orders implicitly. When the eggs reappeared they were as raw as ever, though somewhat warm, and each had its little punctured hole. I took the cook to task and she assured me vociferously that " they broke themselves." Apparently there was some superstition connected with the matter which none dared violate. At any rate I never succeeded in being served un-holed eggs in all rural Honduras.

Not only have these people of the wilderness next to nothing to eat, but they are too indolent to learn to cook what they have. The thick, doughy tortillas and half-boiled black beans, accompanied by black, unstrained coffee with dirty crude sugar and without milk, were not merely monotonous, but would have been fatal to civilized man of sedentary habits. Only the constant toil and sweat, and the clear water of mountain stream offset somewhat the evil effects under which even a horseman would probably have succumbed. The inhabitants of the Honduranean wilds are distinctly less human in their habits than the wild men of the Malay Peninsula. For the latter at least build floors of split bamboo above the ground. Without exaggeration the people of this region were more uncleanly than their gaunt and yellow curs, for the latter carefully picked a spot to lie in while the human beings threw themselves down anywhere and nonchalantly motioned to a guest to sit down or drop his bundle among fresh offal. They literally never washed, except by accident, and handled food and filth alternately with a child-like blandness.

I was just preparing to leave San Juan when a woman came from a neighboring hut to request my assistance at a child-birth! In this region all "gringoes" have the reputation of being physicians, and the inhabitants will not be undeceived. I forcibly tore myself away and struck for the surrounding wilderness.

From soon after noon until sunset I climbed incessantly among tumbled rocks without seeing a human being. A cold wind howled through a vast pine forest of the highest altitude of my Honduranean journey — more than six thousand feet above sea-level. Night fell in wild solitude, but I could only plod on, for to sleep out at this height would have been dangerous. Luckily a corner of moon lighted up weirdly a moderately wide trail. I had tramped an hour or more into the night when a flickering light ahead among the trees showed what might have been a camp of bandits, but which proved to be only that of a group of muleteers, who had stacked their bales of merchandise around three sides under an ancient roof on poles and rolled up in their blankets close to the blazing wood fire they had built to the leeward of it.

They gave no sign of offering me place and I marched on into the howling night. Perhaps four miles beyond I made out a cluster of habitations

A beef just butchered and hung out in the sun

A dwelling on the hot lands of the coast, and its scantily clad inhabitants

pitched on the summit and slope of a hill leaning toward the trail with nothing above it on any side to break the raging wind.   An uproar of barking dogs greeted my arrival, and it was some time before an inmate of one of the dark and silent huts summoned up courage to peer out upon me.   He emerged armed with a huge stick and led the way to a miserable hovel on the hilltop, where he beat on the door and called out that an " hombrecito " sought posada. This opened at last and I entered a mud room in one end of which a fire of sticks blazed fitfully.   A woman of perhaps forty, though appearing much older, as is the case with most women of Honduras, lay on a wooden bed and a girl of ten huddled among rags near the fire.   I asked for food and the woman ordered the girl to heat me black coffee and tortillas. The child was naked to the waist, though the bitter cold wind howled with force through the hut, the walls and especially the gables and roof of which were far from whole.   The woman complained of great pain in her right leg, and knowing she would otherwise groan and howl the night through in the hope of attracting the Virgin's attention, I induced her to swallow two sedative pills.   The smoke made me weep as I swung my hammock from two soot-blackened rafters, but the fire soon went out and I awoke from the first doze shivering until the hut shook.   The temperature was not low compared with our northern winters, but the wind carried a penetrating chill that

reached the marrow of the bones. I rose and tried
unsuccessfully to relight the fire. The half-naked
girl proved more skilful and I sat huddled on a stool
over the fire, alternately weeping with the smoke and
all but falling into the blaze as I dozed. The pills
had little effect on my hostess. I gave her three
more, but her Honduranean stomach was evidently
zinc-lined and she groaned and moaned incessantly.
I returned to my hammock and spent several dream-
months at the North Pole before I was awakened at
first cockcrow by the old woman kneeling on the
earth floor before a lithograph of the Virgin surrounded by withered pine branches, wailing a sing-
song prayer. She left off at length with the information that her only hope of relief was to make a
pilgrimage to the " Virgen de los Remedios," and ordered the girl to prepare coffee. I paid my bill of
two reales and gave the girl one for herself, evidently
the largest sum she had ever possessed, if indeed she
remained long in possession of it after I took my
hobbling and shivering departure.

A cold and wind-swept hour, all stiffly up or down,
brought me to Esperanza, near which I saw the first
wheeled vehicle of Honduras, a contraption of solid
wooden wheels behind gaunt little oxen identical with
those of northwest Spain even to the excruciating
scream of its greaseless axle. In the outskirts two
ragged, hoof-footed soldiers sprang up from behind

Along the Pasoreal river

the bushes of a hillside and came down upon me, waving their muskets and screaming:

" A'onde va? D'onde viene? Have you a pass to go through our department? "

" Yes, from your consul in Guatemala."

They did not ask to read it, perhaps for a reason, but permitted me to pass; to my relief, for the old woman had announced that smallpox was raging in her town of Yamaranguila and its people were not allowed to enter Esperanza. This proved to be a place of considerable size, of large huts scattered over a broad grassy plain in a sheltered valley, with perhaps five thousand inhabitants but not a touch of civilization. Crowds of boys and dirty ragged soldiers followed me, grinning and throwing salacious comments as I wandered from house to house trying to buy food. At a corner of the plaza the comandante called to me from his hut. I treated him with the haughty air of a superior, with frequent reference to my " orders from the government," and he quickly subsided from patronizing insolence to humility and sent a soldier to lead me to " where food is prepared for strangers." Two ancient crones, pottering about a mud stove in an open-work reed kitchen through which the mountain wind swept chillingly, half-cooked an enormous slab of veal, boiled a pot of the ubiquitous black coffee, and scraped together a bit of stale bread, or more exactly cake, for *pan dulce* was the only species that the town afforded. A dish of tomatoes of the size of small cherries proved far more appetizing, after they had been well washed, but the astonishment with which the aged pair watched me eat them suggested that the tradition that held this fruit poison still reigns in Esperanza.

Back once more in the comandancia I resolved to repay the soldiers scattered about town for their insolence in the one way painful to the Honduranean — by making them exert themselves. Displaying again my " government order," I demanded a photograph of the garrison of Esperanza with the comandante, its generals, colonels, lieutenants, and all the lesser fry at the head; and an imperative command soon brought the entire force of fifty or more hurrying barefoot and startled, their ancient muskets under their arms, from the four somnolent corners of the city. I kept them manœuvering a half-hour or so, ostensibly for photographic reasons, while all the populace looked on, and the *reos*, or department prisoners in their chains, formed a languid group leaning on their shovels at the edge of the plaza waiting until their guards should be returned to them.

At ten I reshouldered my stuff and marched out in a still cold, cloudy, upland day, the wondering inhabitants of Esperanza staring awe-stricken after me until I disappeared from view. A few miles out I met two pure Indians, carrying oranges in nets on their backs, the supporting strap across their fore-heads. To my question they admitted the fruit was for sale, though it is by no means uncommon in Central America for countrymen to refuse to sell on the road produce they are carrying to town for that purpose. I asked for a real's worth. Luckily they misunderstood, for the price was "two hands for a medio," and as it was I had to leave lying on the grass several of the ten fine large oranges one of the aborigines had counted on his fingers and accepted a two-and-a-half cent piece for with a "Muchas gracias, amigo." Farther on I met scores of these short, thick-set Indians, of both sexes and all ages, straining along over mountain trails for forty or fifty miles from their colonies to town each with at most a hundred and fifty oranges they would there scarcely sell for so high a price.

Beyond a fordable, ice-cold stream a fairly good road changed to an atrocious mountain trail in a labyrinth of tumbled pine-clad ridges and gullies, on which I soon lost my way in a drizzling rain. The single telegraph wire came to my rescue, jumping lightly from moss-grown stick to tall slender tree-trunk across vast chasms down into and out of which I had to slip and slide and stumble pantingly upward in pursuit. Before dark I was delighted to fall upon a trail again, though not with its condition, for it was generally perpendicular and always thick with loose stones. A band of arrieros cooking their scanty supper under a shelter tent asserted there were houses some two leagues on, but for hours I hobbled over mountains of pure stone, my maltreated feet wincing at every step, without verifying the assertion. Often the descents were so steep I had to pick each footstep carefully in the darkness, and more than one climb required the assistance of my hands. A swift stream all but swept me off my feet, and in the stony climb beyond I lost both trail and telegraph wire and, after floundering about for some time in a swamp, was forced to halt and swing my hammock between two saplings under enormous sheer cliffs that looked like great medieval castles in the night, their white faces spotted by the trees that found foothold on them. Happily I had dropped well down out of the clouds that hover about Esperanza and the cold mountain wind was now much tempered. The white mountain wall rising sheer from my very hips was also somewhat sheltering, though it was easy to dream of rocks being dropped from aloft upon me.

I had clambered a steep and rocky three hours next morning before I came upon the first evidences of humanity, a hut on a little tableland, with all the customary appurtenances and uncleanliness. Black unstrained coffee and tortillas of yellow hue gradually put strength enough to my legs to enable them to push me on through bottomless rocky barrancas, and at length, beyond the hamlet of Santa María,

up one of the highest climbs of the trip to the long
crest of a ridge thick with whispering pines and with
splendid views of the " Great Depths," dense in wood-
land, on either side as far as the eye could reach.
Muleteers passed frequently, often carrying on their
own backs a bundle of the Santa Rosa cigars with
which their animals were laden.   Except for her
soldiers, accustomed to " show off " before their fellows, every person I had met in Honduras had been
kindly and courteous — if dirty — and never with
a hint of coveting my meager hoard.   Beggars seemed
as unknown as robbers — perhaps from lack of initiative and energy.   From Esperanza on, the Indian
boys I met driving mules or carrying nets of oranges
all folded their hands before them like a Buddhist
at prayer when they approached me, but instead of
mumbling some request for alms, as I expected, they
greeted me with an almost obsequious " Adiós " and
a faint smile.   How the " little red schoolhouse " is
lacking in this wooded mountainland!   Not merely
was the immense majority entirely illiterate, but very
few of them had even reached the stage of desiring
to learn.   A paucity of intelligence and initiative
made all intercourse monotonously the same.   The
greeting was never a hearty, individual phrase of the
speaker's own choosing, but always the invariable
" Adiós, Buenos días, tardes or noche," even though
I had already addressed some inquiry to them.   Re-
plies to questions of distance were as stereotyped,

with the diminutive *ito* beloved of the Central Americans tacked on wherever possible:

"Larguita 'stá! A la vueltita no más! Está cerquita! De día no llega! A la tardecita llega. Ay no masito! A la oracióncita llega —"

Nothing could bring them down from these glittering generalities to a definite statement of distance, in leagues or hours, and to reach a place reported "Just around the little corner" was as apt to mean a half day's tramp as that it was over the next knoll.

In the *aldea* of Tutule I fell in with Alberto Suaza, a pleasant appearing, all but white Honduranean, who had once been in the army and was now returning on horseback from some government errand. The hamlet slumbered on a slope of a little leaning valley backed by a wooded mountain ridge, all but a few of the inhabitants being engaged in coffee culture in the communal tract up over the hill when we arrived. Suaza picketed his diminutive animal before the hut of a friend, in which we shared two eggs and coffee and turned in together. Unfortunately I let my companion persuade me against my better judgment to lay aside my hammock and sleep on his " bed," a sun-dried ox-hide thrown on the earth floor, on my side of which, " because he was more used to hard beds than those señores gringoes," he spread most of the *colchón* (mattress) — which consisted of two empty grainsacks. Either these or the painfully thin blanket over us housed a nimble breed I had

miraculously escaped thus far on the journey, robbing me of the much-needed sleep the incessant barking of a myriad of dogs, the itching of mosquito bites,
the rhinoceros-like throat-noises of the family, and
the rock hardness of the floor would probably otherwise have pilfered. The man of the house had
stripped stark naked and, wrapping a red blanket
about him, lay down on a bare wooden bed to pass
the night apparently in perfect comfort. Soft mortals indeed are we of civilized and upholstered lands.

Suaza made no protest when I paid the bill for
both, and by seven we were off, he riding his tiny
horse until we were out of sight of the town, then
dismounting to lead it the rest of the day. He had
announced himself the possessor of an immensely
rich aunt on whose hacienda we should stop for
" breakfast," and promised we should spend the night
either in the gold mine of which she was a chief stock-
holder or at her home in La Paz, which I gathered to
be a great mansion filled with all the gleanings of that
lady's many trips to Europe and the States. I had
long since learned the Latin American's love of personal exaggeration. But Suaza was above the Honduranean average; he not only read with comparative ease but cleaned his finger nails, and I looked forward with some eagerness to a coming oasis of civilization in the hitherto unsoftened wilderness.

It was an ideal day for tramping, cloudy yet
bright, with a strong fresh wind almost too cold

for sitting still and across a country green and fragrant with endless forest, and after the climb back of Tutule little more than rolling. It was noon before we came upon the new mud-and-tiled house of the cattle-tender of " dear aunty's " hacienda, and though the meal we enjoyed there was savory by Honduranean standards, it was not so completely Parisian as I had permitted myself to anticipate. That I was allowed to pay for it proved nothing, for the employees of the wealthy frequently show no aversion to accepting personal favors.

Not far beyond we came out on the edge of a tableland with a splendid view of the valley of Comayagua, far below, almost dead level, some ten miles wide and thirty long, deep green everywhere, with cloud shadows giving beautiful color effects across it in the jumble of green mountains with the purple tinge of distance beyond which lay Tegucigalpa. At the same time there began the most laborious descent of the journey, an utterly dry mountain face pitched at an acute angle and made up completely of loose rock, down which we must pick every step and often use our hands to keep from landing with broken bones at the bottom. The new buildings of the mine were in plain sight almost directly below us from the beginning, yet we were a full two hours in zigzagging by short legs straight down the loose-stone slope to them. The American

The mozo pauses for a drink on the trail

One way of transporting merchandise from the coast to Tegucigalpa

manager was absent, but in the general store of the company I had not only the pleasure of spending an hour in the first thoroughly clean building I had seen in Honduras, but of speaking English, for the two Negro youths in charge of the place were natives of Belize, or British Honduras, and were equally fluent in my own tongue or Spanish, while their superiority in personal condition over the natives was a sad commentary on the boasted advantage of the republican form of government.

The thirsty, rock-sown descent continued, bringing us at last with aching thighs to the level of the vast valley, more than four thousand feet below the lodging-places of the few days past. Suaza mounted his horse and prepared to enter his native La Paz in style. So often had kingly quarters promised me by the self-styled sons of wealth in Latin America gradually degenerated to the monotonous tortilla level of general conditions that I had not been able entirely to disabuse myself of an expectation of disappointment. Such enough, where the trail broke up into a score of paths among mud huts and pig wallows, my companion paused in the dark to say:

" Perhaps after all it will be better to take you right to my house for to-night. One always feels freer in one's father's house. My aunt might be holding some social affair, or be sick or — But we will surely call at her mansion to-morrow, and —"

"Como usted quiera?" I answered, swallowing my disappointment. At least his father's house should be something above the ordinary.

But to my astonishment we stopped a bit farther on in the suburbs before one of the most miserable mud hovels it had been my misfortune to run across in Honduras, swarming with pigs, yellow curs, and all the multitudinous filth and disarray indigenous to the country. The coldest of welcomes greeted us, the frowsy, white-bearded father in the noisome doorway replying to the son's query of why there was no light with a crabbed:

"If you want light why don't you come in the day-time?"

My companion told a boy of the family to go buy a candle, and his scrawny, unkempt mother bounded out of the hut with the snarl of a miser:

"What do you want a candle for?"

The boy refused to go and Suaza tied his horse to a bush and went in quest of one himself.   I mentioned supper, hinting at my willingness to pay for anything that could be furnished, but to each article I suggested came the monotonous, indifferent Honduranean answer, "No hay."   After much growling and an extended quarrel with her son, the woman set on a corner of a wabbly-legged table, littered with all manner of unsavory junk, two raw eggs, punctured and warmed, a bowl of hot water and a stale slab of *pan dulce*, a cross between poor bread and

worse cake. I wandered on into the town in the
hope of finding some imitation of a hotel. But
though the place had a population of several thousand, it was made up exclusively of mud huts only
two or three of which were faintly lighted by pine-
splinters. The central plaza was a barren, un-
lighted pasture, a hut on the corner of which was reputed to be a shop, but when I had beaten my way
into it I found nothing for sale except bottles of an
imitation wine at monopoly prices. In my disgust
I pounded my way into every hovel that was said to
be a tienda. Not an edible thing was to be found.
One woman claimed to have fruit for sale, and after
collecting a high price for them she went out into
the patio and picked a half-dozen perfectly green
oranges.

" But what do people eat and drink in La Paz?
Grass and water? " I demanded.

But the bedraggled population was not even amen-
able to crude sarcasm, and the only reply I got was
a lazy, child-like:

" Oh, each one keeps what he needs to eat in his
own house."

Here was a town of a size to have been a place of
importance in other lands, yet even the mayor lived
with his pigs on an earth floor. Statistics of population have little meaning in Honduras. The place
recalled a cynical " gringo's " description of a similar town, " It has a hundred men, two hundred

women, and 100,000 chuchos "— the generic term in
Central America for yellow curs of all colors.   Why
every family houses such a swarm of these miserable
beasts is hard to guess.   Mere apathy, no doubt, for
they are never fed; nor, indeed, are the pigs that also
overrun every household and live, like the dogs, on
the offal of the patio or backyard that serves as place
of convenience.   They have at least the doubtful
virtue of partly solving the sewer problem, which is
not a problem to Honduraneans.   A tortilla or other
food held carelessly is sure to be snatched by some
cat, pig, or dog; a bundle left unwatched for a moment is certain to be rooted about the floor or de-
posited with filth.   These people utterly lack any
notion of improvement.   A child or an animal, for
instance, climbs upon the table or into a dish of food.
When the point is reached at which it is unavoidable,
the person nearest shouts, throws whatever is handy,
or kicks at the offender; but though the same identical performance is repeated a score of times during
a single meal, there is never any attempt to correct
the culprit, to drive it completely off, or remove the
threatened dish from the danger zone.   A people in-
habiting a land that might be a garden spot of the
earth drift through their miserable lives in identically
the same fashion as their gaunt and mangy curs.

There was a great gathering of the neighboring
cleans in the Suaza hut next morning, while my companion of the day before enlarged upon what he

The other way of bringing goods up to the capital

The garrison of Amapala

fancied he knew about his distinguished guest. Among those who crowded the place were several men of education, in the Honduranean sense,— about equal to that of a poorly trained American child in the fourth grade. But there was not one of them that did not show a monkey curiosity and irresponsibility in handling every article in my pack; my sweater — "Ay qué lindo!" my papers —"How beautiful!" an extremely ordinary shirt —"How soft and fine! How costly!" and "How much did this cost? — and that?" Suaza displayed my medicine-case to the open-mouthed throng — and would I give mother some pills for her colic, and would I please photograph each one of the family — and so on to the end of patience. There was no mention made of the wealthy aunt and her mansion after the day dawned. The invitation to spend a few days, " as many as you like," amid the luxuries of Paris and the Seven Seas had tapered down to the warmed eggs and black coffee, the only real food I ate being that I had bought in a house-to-house canvass in the morning. I had distributed pills to most of the family and several neighbors and photographed them, at the request of the man of many promises, had paid his bills on the road since our meeting; while I prepared my pack, he requested me to send him six prints each of the pictures, some postals of New York, a pair of pajamas such as I carried, " and any other little things I might think he would like," including long weekly letters, and as I rose to take my leave and asked what I owed him, he replied with a bland and magnanimous smile:

"You owe me nothing whatever, señor,— only to mamá," and dear mamá collected about what a first-class hotel would have for the same length of time.

CHAPTER X

THE CITY OF THE SILVER HILLS

A MONOTONOUS wide path full of loose stones led through dry, breathless jungle across the valley floor to Comayagua. The former capital of the republic had long held a place in my imagination, and the distant view of it the day before from the lofty rim of the valley backed by long blue ranges of mountains had enhanced my desire to visit the place, even though it lay somewhat off the direct route. But romance did not long survive my entrance. For the most part it was merely a larger collection of huts along badly cobbled or grass-grown streets common to all " cities " of Honduras. A stub-towered, white-washed cathedral, built by the Spaniards and still the main religious edifice of Honduras, faced the drowsy plaza; near it were a few " houses of commerce," one-story plaster buildings before which hung a sign with the owner's name and possibly some hint of his business, generally that of hawking a few bolts of cloth, straw hats, or ancient and fly-specked cheap products from foreign parts. The town boasted a place that openly receives travelers, but its two canvas cots and its rafters were already occupied by several snobbish and gawkily dressed young natives bound from the north coast to the capital.

The chief of telegraphs finally led me to the new billard-hall, where a lawyer in a frock coat and the manners of a prime minister admitted he had an empty shop in which I could swing my hammock. When he had finished his game, he got a massive key and a candle and led the way in person to a small hut in a side street, the rafters uncomfortably high above the tile floor, on which I was fortunate to have a newspaper to spread before depositing my bundle. The lawyer took leave of me with the customary "At your orders; here you are in your own house," and marched ministerially away with the several pompous friends who had accompanied him. But a few moments later, having shaken them off, he returned to collect ten cents — one real for rent and another for the candle. It was the first lodging I had paid since leaving Guatemala City. As I doubled up in my ill-hung hammock, the dull thump of a distant guitar and the explosion of a rare fire-cracker broke the stillness of New Year's eve, while now and then there drifted to my ears the sound of a band in the main plaza that tortured the night at intervals into the small hours.

Comayagua by day was a lazy, silent place, chiefly barefoot, the few possessors of shoes being gaudily dressed young men whose homes were earth-floored

Marooned "gringoes" waiting with what patience possible at the "Hotel Morazan," Amapala

Unloading cattle in the harbor of Amapala

huts.   The place had the familiar Central-American air of trying to live with the least possible exertion; its people were a mongrel breed running all the gamut from black to near-white.   There were none of the fine physical specimens common to the highlands of Mexico, and the teeth were notably bad.   A few of the soldiers, in blue-jean uniforms with what had once been white stripes, faded straw hats, and bare feet, were mountain Indians with well-developed chests; for military service — of the catch-them-with-a-rope variety — is compulsory in Honduras.   But the population in general was anemic and stunted. Two prisoners were at work in the streets; more properly they sat smoking cigarettes and putting a finger cautiously to their lips when I passed in silent request not to wake up their guard, who was sound asleep on his back in the shade, his musket lying across his chest.   The town had one policeman, a kinky-haired youth in a white cap and a pale light gray cotton uniform, who carried a black club and wore shoes!   The *cartero*, or mailman, was a barefoot boy in faded khaki and an ancient straw hat, who wandered lazily and apparently aimlessly about town with the week's correspondence in hand, reading the postals and feeling the contents of each letter with a proprietary air.   The sun was brilliant and hot here in the valley, and there was an aridity that had not been suggested in the view of it from the heights above.

It was no place to spend New Year's, however, stiff and sore though I was from the hardships of the road, and toward lazy, silent noonday I wandered on along the trail to the modern capital, hoping that it, at least, might have real beds and a hotel, and perhaps even white inhabitants. The battered old church bells were thumping as I topped the slight rise that hid the town from view, and it was four hours later that I saw or heard the next human being, or any other evidence of his existence except a stretch of barb-wire and one lone telegraph wire sagging from one crooked stick to another. The four stony dry but flat leagues along the valley floor had brought me to San Antonio, all the population of which was loafing and mildly celebrating New Year's, as they would celebrate any other possible excuse not to work. Here I obtained water, and new directions that led me off more toward the east and the heaped-up mountains that lay between me and Tegucigalpa. On all sides spread a dry, bushy land, aching for cultivation. I had the good fortune to fall in with a river so large I was able to swim three strokes in one of its pools, and strolled with dusk into the town of Flores on the edge of the first foothills of the ranges still to be surmounted.

Though still a lazy naked village, this one showed some hint of the far-off approach of civilization. Animals were forbidden the house in which I passed the night, and its tile-floor was almost clean. This latter virtue was doubly pleasing, for the rafters above were so high that even when I had tied my hammock by the very ends of the ropes I could only climb in by mounting a chair and swinging myself up as into a trapeze; and if I must break a leg it would be some slight compensation to do so on a clean floor. How much uncleanliness this simple little 30-cent net had kept me up out of since the day I bought it in Guatemala City!

Like many of the tasks of life, this one grew easier toward its termination. A moderate day's walk, not without rocky climbs and *bajadas*, but with considerable stretches of almost level going across solitary wind-cooled plains, brought me to Támara. A passing company of soldiers had all but gutted the village larder, but at dusk in the last hut I got not only food but meat, and permission to swing my hammock from the blackened rafters of the reed kitchen, over the open pots and pans. Incidentally, for the first time in Honduras prices were quadrupled in honor of my being a foreigner. Civilization indeed was approaching.

Half way up the wooded ridge beyond I met the sun mounting from the other side, fell in soon after with a real highway, and at eleven caught the first sight of Tegucigalpa, the " City of the Silver Hills," capital of the Sovereign and Independent Republic of Honduras. It was no very astounding sight; merely what in other lands would have been considered a

large village, a chiefly one-story place with a white-
washed church, filling only a small proportion of a
somewhat barren valley surrounded by high rocky
and partly wooded hills. I marched down through
Comayagüela in all the disreputableness of fifteen
days on the trail, across the little bridge of a few
arches over a shallow river which to Honduraneans
far and wide is one of the greatest works of man, and
into the park-like little central plaza, with its arbor
of huge purple bourgainvillea.

The " Hotel Jockey Club " was not all that the
imagination might have pictured, but at least there
was the satisfaction of knowing that any stranger
in town, be he "gringo " or president-elect, famous
or infamous, rich or honest, could stop nowhere else.
Among its luxuries was a " bath," which turned out
to be a massive stone vessel in the basement with a
drizzle of cold water from a faucet above that was
sure to run dry about the time the victim was well
soaped; its frontiersman rooms were furnished with
little more than weak-kneed canvas cots, and the barefoot service of the dining-room was assisted by all
the dogs, fowls, and flies of the region. But there
lay two hungry weeks of Central American trail
behind me and for days to come I ate unquestioningly
anything that came within reach of my fingers, of
whatever race, color, or previous condition of servi-
tude.

Just around the corner — as everything is in this

miniature capital — the American Legation delivered
the accumulated mail of a month, and the pair of real
shoes I had had the happy thought of sending to myself here months before. This bit of foresight saved
me from hobbling on to the coast barefoot. I had
arrived just in time to attend one of Tegucigalpa's
gala events, the inspection of her newly reformed
police force. " It is set for three," said the legation
secretary, " so come around about three-thirty."
Just around another corner we entered toward four
the large dusty patio of a one-story building of mud
blocks, against the adobe wall of which were lined
up something over a hundred half-frightened, half-
proud Honduranean Indians in brand new, dark-blue
uniforms and caps, made in Germany, and armed with
black night-sticks and large revolvers half-hidden in
immense holsters. We took the places of honor re-
served for us at a bench and table under the patio
veranda beside the chief of police, an American
soldier of fortune named Lee Christmas. He was a
man nearing fifty, totally devoid of all the embroidery
of life, golden toothed and graying at the temples,
but still hardy and of youthful vigor, of the dress
and manner of a well-paid American mechanic, who
sat chewing his black cigar as complacently as if he
were still at his throttle on the railroad of Guatemala.
Following the latest revolution he had reorganized
what, to use his own words, had been " a bunch of
barefooted apes in faded-blue cotton rags " into the

solemn military company that was now to suffer its
first formal inspection. The native secretary, standing a bit tremulously in the edge of the shade, called
from the list in his hand first the name of Christmas
himself, then that of the first assistant, and his own,
he himself answering " present " for each of these.
Next were the commanders, clerks, under-secretaries,
and the like in civilian garb, each, as his name was
pronounced, marching past us hat in hand and bowing profoundly. Last came the policemen in uniform. As the secretary read his title and first name,
each self-conscious Indian stepped stiffly forth from
the ranks, throwing a foot, heavy with the unac-
customed shoe, high in the air and pounding the earth
in the new military style taught him by a willowy
young native in civilian dress who leaned haughtily
on his cane watching every movement, made a sharp-
cornered journey about the sun-flooded yard and
bringing up more or less in front of his dreaded
chief, gave a half turn, raised the right leg to the
horizontal with the grace of an aged ballet dancer
long since the victim of rheumatism, brought it down
against the left like the closing of a heavy trap-
door, saluted with his night-stick and huskily called
out his own last name, which Christmas checked off
on the list before him without breaking the thread of
the particular anecdote with which he chanced at
that moment to be entertaining us.

" I tried to get 'em to cut out this —— —— German monkey business of throwing their feet around," confided the chief sadly, " but it 's no use, for it 's in the —— —— military manual."

Judged by Central-American standards the force was well trained.   But the poor Indians and half-breeds that made up its bulk were so overwhelmed with the solemnity of the extraordinary occasion that they were even more ox-like in their clumsiness and nearer frightened apes in demeanor than in their native jungles.   The quaking fear of making a mis-step caused them to keep their eyes riveted on the lips of our compatriot, from which, instead of the words of wrath they no doubt often imagined, issued some such remark as:

" Why —— —— it, W——, one of the bums I picked up along the line one day in Guatemala told me the best —— —— yarn that —"

Nor could they guess that the final verdict on the great ceremony that rang forth on the awe-struck silence as the chief rose to his feet was:

" Well, drop around to my room in the hotel when you want to hear the rest of it.   But if you see the sign on my door, ' Ladies Only To-day,' don't knock. The chambermaid may not have finished her official visit."

The climate of Tegucigalpa leaves little to be de-sired.   Otherwise it is merely a large Central-Ameri-can village of a few thousand inhabitants, with much of the indifference, uncleanliness, and ignorance of the rest of the republic. Priests are numerous, wandering about smoking their cigarettes and protected from the not particularly hot sun by broad hats and umbrellas. One lonely little native sheet masquerades as a newspaper, the languid little shops, often owned by foreigners, offer a meager and ancient stock chiefly imported and all high in price; for it takes great inducement to make the natives produce anything beyond the corn and beans for their own requirements. The "national palace" is a green, clap-boarded building, housing not only the president and his little reception-room solemn with a dozen chairs in cotton shrouds, but congress, the ministry, and the "West Point of Honduras," the superintendent of which was a native youth who had spent a year or two at Chapultepec. Against it lean barefooted, anemic " soldiers " in misfit overalls, armed with musket and bayonet that overtop them in height. The main post-office of the republic is an ancient adobe hovel, in the cobwebbed recesses of which squat a few stupid fellows waiting for the mule-back mail-train to arrive that they may lock up in preparation for beginning to look over the correspondence mañana. It is not the custom to make appointments in Tegucigalpa. If one resident desires the presence of another at dinner, or some less excusable function, he wanders out just before the hour set until he picks up his guest somewhere. By night the town is doubly dead. The shops put up

their wooden shutters at dusk, the more energetic
inhabitants wander a while about the cobbled streets,
dim-lighted here and there by arc-lights, the cathedral bells jangle at intervals like suspended pieces of
scrap-iron, arousing a chorus of barking dogs, and a
night in which two blankets are comfortable settles
down over all the mountainous, moon-flooded region.
There is not even the imitation of a theater, the plaza
concert on Sunday evenings, in which the two sexes
wander past each other in opposite directions for
an hour or two, being the only fixed recreation.   A
man of infinite patience, or who had grown old and
weary of doing, might find Tegucigalpa agreeable;
but it would soon pall on the man still imbued with
living desires.

The fitting shield of Honduras would be one bearing as motto that monotonous phrase which greets
the traveler most frequently along her trails, " No
hay."   The country is noted chiefly for what " there
is not."   Everywhere one has the impression of
watching peculiarly stupid children playing at being a republic.   The nation is a large farm in size
and a poorly run one in condition.   The wave of
" liberty " that swept over a large part of the world
after the French Revolution left these wayward and
not over-bright inhabitants of what might be a rich
and fertile land to play at governing themselves, to
ape the forms of real republics, and mix them with
such childish clauses as come into their infantile

minds. The chief newspaper of the republic resembles a high-school periodical, concocted by particularly thick-headed students without faculty assistance or editing. A history of their childish governmental activities would fill volumes. In 1910 all the copper one-centavo coins were called in and crudely changed to two-centavo pieces by surcharging the figure 2 and adding an s, a much smaller one-centavo coin being issued. The " government " may have made as much as $50 by the transaction. Not long before my arrival, the current postage-stamps, large quantities of which had been bought by foreign firms within the country, were suddenly declared worthless, and the entire accumulated correspondence for the next steamer returned to the senders, instead of at least being forwarded to destination under excess charges. Foreigners established the first factory Tegucigalpa had ever known, which was already employing a half-hundred of the pauperous inhabitants in the making of candles, when the " government " suddenly not only put a heavy duty on stearine but required the payment of back duty on all that had already been imported. An Englishman came down from the mines of San Juancito embued with the desire to start a manual-training school in the capital. He called on the mulatto president and offered his services free for a year, if the government would invest $5000 in equipment. The president told him to come back mañana. On that elusive day he was informed that the government had no such sum at its disposal.

" I have saved up $2500 myself," replied the Englishman, " which I will lend the government for the purpose, if it will add a like amount."

But when mañana came again, the president expressed his regrets that the national treasury could not endure such a strain.

The best view of Tegucigalpa is had from Picacho, a long ridge from back in the mountains, ending in a blunt nose almost sheer above the city. Whoever climbs it recognises the reason for the native saying, " He who holds Picacho sleeps in the palace." Its town-side face is almost precipitous, and on every hand spread rolling, half-bare upland mountains. All but sheer below, in the lowest depression of the visible world, sits the little capital, rather compact in the center, then scattered along the little river and in the suburb of Comayagüela beyond it. The dull-red tile roofs predominate, and the city is so directly below that one can see almost to the bottom of every tree-grown patio. A few buildings are of two stories, and the twin-towers of the little white cathedral stand somewhat above the general level. But most noticeable of any is the fact that all the vast broken plain surrounding it far and wide lies almost entirely uncultivated, for the most part neither cleared nor inhabited, crossed by several roads and trails, most conspicuous of all the two white ribbons by one of which I had arrived from the north and the other of which was already inviting me onward to the coast and new climes.

A fellow-gringo, bound for the Pacific exit on a miniature horse, packed away my baggage on his cargo mule and left me to walk unhampered. A highway some fifty feet wide and white with dust struck off uncertainly toward the southwest, a splendid highway once, built for automobiles by the combined efforts of the government and an American mining company farther up in the hills, but now suffered to fall here and there into a disrepair that made it as useless for such traffic as a mountain trail. The first day of thirty miles brought us to Sabana Grande, with a species of hotel. During the second, there were many down-grade short-cuts, full of loose stones and dusty dry under the ever warmer sun, with the most considerable bridge in Honduras over the Pasoreal River, and not a few stiff climbs to make footsore my entrance into the village of Pespire. Here was a house that frankly and openly displayed the sign "Restaurante," in a corner of which travelers of persuasive manners might be furnished *tijeras*, sissor-legged canvas cots on which to toss out the night; for Pespire is far below Tegucigalpa and on the edge of the blazing tropics.

For which reason we rose at three to finish the half-day of sea-level country left us. The stars hung brilliant and a half moon lighted up a way that was

The steamer arrives at last that is to carry us south to Panama

We lose no time in being rowed out to her

hot even at this hour. From sunrise on huge lizards
scurried up among the wayside rocks as we passed,
and sat torpid, staring at us with their lack-luster
eyes. Natives wearing spurs on their hoof-like bare
feet rode by us now and then, and mule-trains or
screaming wooden carts crawled past on their way
up to the capital. All traffic between Tegucigalpa
and the outside world passes either over this route
or the still longer trail from Puerto Cortez, on the
north coast, from which a toy railroad limps a few
miles inland before losing its courage and turning
back. By daylight the fantastic ranges of the interior had disappeared and the last low foothill soon
left us to plod on straight across a dust-dry sandy
plain with brown withered grass and mesquite bushes,
among which panted scores of cattle. Honduras
runs so nearly down to a point on its Pacific side
that the mountains of both Salvador and Nicaragua
stood out plainly to the right and left.

By sweltering ten we were swimming in the Pacific
before the scattered village of San Lorenzo, though
there was visible only a little arm of the sea shut in
by low bushy islands. It was our good fortune not
to have to charter by telegraph and at the expense
of a Honduranean fortune means of transportation
to the island port of Amapala; for before we could
seek the shelter of our sun-faded garments a launch
put in for a party that had been forming for several
days past. The passengers included a shifty-eyed

old priest in charge of two nuns, the rules of whose order forbade them to speak to men, and the mozo of an influential Honduranean who had shot a man the night before and was taking advantage of his master's personal friendship with the judge of the district. The launch wound between bushy banks and came out at last on a rich-blue bay shut off in the far distance by several jagged black volcanic islands, toward one of which it wheezed a hot and monotonous three hours. This was "Tiger's Island," named evidently from the one moth-eaten specimen that had once been landed here by a passing circus. At a narrow wooden wharf of this we at length gradually tied up. Ragged, barefoot soldiers stopped us to write our pedigrees, as if we were entering some new country, and addressed us in monkey signs instead of the Spanish of which experience had convinced them all traveling foreigners were ignorant.

Amapala is a species of outdoor prison to which all travelers to or from Honduras on the Pacific side are sentenced for a term varying in length according to their luck, which is generally bad. Those who do not sleep in the park toss out their imprisonment on a bedstead of woven ropes in a truly Honduranean building that disguises itself under the name of "Hotel Morazan," the slatternly keeper of which treats her helpless inmates with the same consideration as any other prison warden devoid of humanity or oversight.   The steamer I awaited was due before I arrived, but day after day I lay marooned on the blazing volcanic rock without a hint as to its whereabouts.   Not even exercise was possible, unless one cared to race up and down the sharp jagged sides of the sea-girt volcano.   The place ranks high as an incubator of malignant fevers and worse ailments, and to cap the climax the ice-machine was broken down.   It always is, if the testimony of generations of castaways is to be given credence.   Our only available pastime was to buy a soap-boxful of oysters, at the cost of a quarter, and sit in the narrow strip of shade before the "hotel" languidly opening them with the only available corkscrew, our weary gaze fixed on the blue arm of water framed by the shimmering hot hills of Salvador by which tradition had it ocean craft sometimes came to the rescue.

But all things have an end, even life imprisonment, and with the middle of January we awoke one morning to find a steamer anchored in the foreground of the picture that had seared itself into our memories. All day long half-naked natives waded lazily back and forth from the beach to the clumsy tenders, exchanging the meager products of the country for ill-packed merchandise from my own.   Night settled down over their unfinished task, the self-same moon came out and the woven-rope cots again creaked and groaned under unwilling guests.   But by noon next day we had swung our hammocks under the awning of the forecastlehead and were off along the tropical blue Pacific for Panama.

THE END